Sex Files

Selem Demwuth

DEDICATION

To Huriya. To us...

CONTENTS

PREFACE

The world is still replete with sexy men: sexy spirit, sexy mind, sexy soul and sexy body: sexy. There is still a plethora of women who are real queens: real queen spirit, mind, soul and body: queen.

Sex Files is a comprehensive glance at our sex state of affairs, our sex worlds and our sexuality. Most of us hold our own truths to be so dear that we sex who, what, how and when we want. If this scenario worked, we'd be in a better position sexually as a human race.

Nevermind the raw parts of Sex Files where we are trying to work it out. If it's not you, it's someone else's story. The collective "we" and "us" may not always apply to all of us. The intent is not a guilt trip, a judgment nor an accusation.

Sex Files is intended to present us with our current sex crises and challenge us to be better about being the humanity that we are. The present culture is so full of my-way, there is no room for what-about-us. There still is an "us". Anyone is allowed to tell their sex stories if that is what they want to do. It is not so much the stories we tell but the heart of our storytellers. Many victims are driven to the public forum to tell such private stories because their perpetrator or perpetrators would not hear them otherwise.

There are sexual justice agendas, hashtags and organizations that are noble or started that way. There are others. Agendas are beautiful. We all have at least one, even if we don't know that we have one. It is one thing to require good humanity of us. It is another to kill him to get "good" humanity out of him; or to kill her to get her to be "good".

The real passion of Sex Files is rooted in the fact that we are sex royalty in a good way. We are the image of an incomparable lover. Sex Files is an invitation to live from there. Love and sex from a love story so grand defies our gender gaps, our personal opinions, our sex vibe.

We all have a greatness. If we can find it and do it, we would defy human reason. Get up higher!

We continue to address the various aspects of our current sex pandemic but we have yet to address it in an honest and comprehensive way. Suddenly men are being dragged to the gallows to be hung for what societies tolerated for thousands of years. Political sex wars are rampant with explosive details to take out Candidate X so that the other power scheme can "rule the kingdom". Hollywood? Well, ... as our heroes go, so we go. Who's your hero?

CHAPTER 1
YOU'RE NOT NAKED

Sex is perfection. Sex is thoroughly beautiful.

Your sex je ne se quoi is an expression of your world. It is not your world nor who you are. Like a thermometer to temperature, so is sex to the human heart.

A thermometer is an indicator. Sex is an indicator.

Some of our hearts are so frickin' beautiful. Beauty is relative but it isn't. Beauty is all good. Some of our hearts are more defined by the places we've been and what happened there. DNA drives the heart as deftly as a Rolls Royce hugs a curve. Occasionally, some of us have a life event so jarring and indelible, it changes the course of our lives. Some of us never get back to "normal"; others, "overcome" enough to get back "on course".

If we took a bird's eye view of our life and our sex universe, we could understand better why we sex that way. Sex is not just our sex performance. It is our entire individual cosmos on sex. We can possibly relate our life world and our sex world.

CAVEAT: There is a life world that surpasses mere existence.

Some of us have a life world that taps extraordinary. Our sex world follows suit. From here – extraordinary life world – you're not naked. Sex is nonpareil in every way.

Naked is our perspective - our limits: our world: our shame places we fight relentlessly to hide. Most of us still live from Naked. Most of us live from here ...

Life World: I've lived like this.

Sex World: I sex like this because I've lived like this. I don't sex like this just because I like to do it this way. My life path has been a journey of living that has brought me to here. My sex world is a product of that journey.

Occasionally, the way we sex may deviate from our sex je ne sais quoi. It is not a sex event of which we speak. It is our sex soul. The way we sex tells much of the story of our life world; for some, our sex bent tells the whole story. The way we sex includes our sex opinions and passions: not just sex physicality. Is it a masterpiece or a tragedy? Is it deliciously impressive and influential, or is it din?

Sex is not grotesque. It is not nasty. It is not dirty. It is not bad. Whatever our labels, they are labels. They may affect the way we perceive sex but labels do not change the inherent good that sex is. They may help us feel more hot and heavy, lit, badass or seductive, but they are not sex.

Our abuse of sex does not change it to our perceptions of it. Our ghastly sexual experiences and inappropriate sexual encounters do not change sex. The product is not flawed. Sometimes a manufacturer makes a mistake: not this one. There are ways to use any product. There may be a certain demographic for the product while another is not suited for it. Very few of us read the manual before we try to use something. Sex has a "manual". Most of us figure it out as we go along or just go along.

Our sex point-of-view is not limited to the world of our five senses. It is our now, our tomorrow, our yesterdays. It is our life force within and without. It is the forces outside of us that we cannot see with our five senses. It is the devious power, the tainted glory, the greed, the hate. Or it is the love, the influence, the wealth, the success.

Unfortunately, there are too many of us who see sex as just sex. There is always an invitation to discover sex – the kingdom. Whether we abuse the Kingdom of Sex or respect it, it is on our stages. Scroll the headlines, follow the hashtags or look around you – we've committed treason with the Kingdom of Sex. Occasionally, very occasionally, we see the terribly sexy power player that Sex is. Sexy Sex like this is the rhythm of a heart that beats just as sexy.

The human heart isn't so much about feelings as it is about why we feel that way. And the why we feel a certain way is engrained in the culture of something. That something has its own roots, belief systems and laws. It is a kingdom, really. The kingdom has a king.

CHAPTER 2
SEX – THE KINGDOM

Big, sexy Sex Kingdom is superfluous with so much damn voluptuous pleasure, sex is like rare luxury: not scarce, unprecedented. Sex emanates from the source. The source is a super lover who is preeminent, extreme, pure. This super lover is radiant with his love of pleasure: transcendent with his take on abundance. In other words, no one can beat the one who orchestrated sex at the pleasure plethora.

Fundamentally, we are limited to love at super lover level. There is an interplay with a superlative love and the human soul to be able to love her at this level; to love him like that. We can tap such love to love our lover with it but we have to "level higher". This superlative love transcends our limited human love capacity. It transcends the best of human love capacities. It is from here that we sex – Sex Kingdom sex. It is from here that we are intimate with the world of sex (not our rendition of it) – sex. Even when we come away to our mere human places, sex is thoroughly beautiful.

A flawless diamond is a flawless diamond. Our greed to get it does not change it. Our jealousy of the "lucky" She wearing the flawless bling does not change it. Our manipulation of its market value does not change it.

Sex is sex. Our games don't change sex. Our sex tapes do not change it. Our inexperience does not change sex. If we're only in it (the relationships) for formalities or the sex, our relationship whys do not define sex. Neither does our political sex wars, booty calls, sex texts, childhood experiences, hashtags, and nude pic wars.

The battles of the sexes that we've waged and continue to wage are implicit attacks on sex whether intentional or unintentional. The sex wars are so corrupt, we sully the sexiest pleasure lovers can ever have. This attack on sex kills the fire of mediocre lovers. There is absolutely nothing wrong with sexy volupt sex. The fault is in our agendas, our methods, our means. The fault is in us. We are flawed; the sex is thoroughly beautiful.

We have action superheroes that do such amazing feats, they exceed human capability and can take on otherworldly powers. Love like this is a love superhero. Love like this is incomparable to the rarest and most costly premium wine. What intoxicates you like a wine that makes you giddy and makes you forget? She is livid for her man to kiss her if he is imbued with this level of love. If he is a conduit for love like this, he can kiss her.

And perhaps, we settle too much. We settle for lovers that are less: for love that is less.

"Oh, how unrealistic!" you say.

If you believe love like this is unrealistic, it is. Some of us are not in it for the love. But, for the rest of the love dreamers, the looming question ever is, "How do I become a lover like that? How do I not settle for anything less?" It helps to know the lover. It helps to know the lover whose love is incomparable to the most rare and costly. It helps to know the lover's sex principle. You are royalty. Even your sex thing is supposed to be the culture of the kingdom of sex. What do you have? Do you have a capacity for love that produces a sex melodrama so uncanny even the love critics and love haters want it? Capacity is more than space. Capacity is heart. Capacity is receptivity. Capacity is culture. Tap your royal self and sex like that.

We cannot continue to settle for all of these lesser loves and expect to get Sex Kingdom sex. The currency of the Kingdom of Sex is serious, bodacious love.

Sex is royalty too. Most of us can process that sex has a certain nobility (a certain superiority), especially compared to our other Others. Some of us have no respect for sex other than it gives us a fleeting high. We jones for as many 2-minute highs a night as we can get. For those exasperated with the disappointing 30-second climax, we seek out other (more lasting) highs.

You are Sex Kingdom royalty. What are you settling for? Big sexy Sex Kingdom sex is not an illusion. A sideliner can hardly be in the game like the players. Sex Kingdom sex players enjoy the game. Oh, don't you dare come to the Sex Kingdom of sexy sex with your rules, unless they happen to be Sex Kingdom's rules. You will only mess up the sex. Voila! That is what we have with our Sex Crises. If you ever come to the big leagues of Sex Kingdom sex and play its game you cannot help but enjoy sexy sex.

Enjoy! Enjoy Enjoy Enjoy! Jouir de! Disfrutar! Apreciar! Ka aanand len! Godere! Qing xiangyong! GenieBen! Naslazhdat'sya!

You must be vested! Love the one you're with. He may not be your endgame. She may be a love trainer. Go for broke on love!

[CAVEAT: If physical, mental, psychological or emotional issues steal your sex pleasure and you want it, seek it out: even if you have to go to the designer of sexy sex to get it.]

CHAPTER 3
SEX GOLD VS SEX ALLOYS

Sex has its own glory. Just like money, beauty, power and strength, it owns its own glory. We cannot disrespect glory without consequence. We cannot contaminate sex with our agendas and not have consequences.

We've missed the art of love and the art of loving. In so doing, the sex is shitty for so many of us. The best of good sex comes from good love: good loving. He can rock your world from here to the moon and back. Your world has officially been rocked, that's all. She can make you walk the ceiling with killer sex: walk fast or take your time.

The problem with sex that does not come from love, is that it comes from somewhere else. It is like mixing gold with other. It devalues the gold and robs other of its ability to be used for its ultimate good. The silver-maker made it that way to fulfill a certain purpose; the gold-maker too. Gold with anything else is gold with "impurities" no matter how luxurious its impurities.

There are no shortfalls in the Kingdom of Sex if you are fully vested. There is only living the voluptuous life.

Voluptuous: pleasure.

Voluptuous: luxury.

Voluptuous: delight.

Voluptuous: finery.

And sometimes the precursor to voluptuous sex is a day of exceptional foreplay: a night of caress or listening to a heartbeat – listen. Sometimes it is a lifetime of learning and living the art of loving. The art of loving is about heart. Are you in with all your heart or is it just about the sex?

We've mixed sex with so many alloys – agendas, personas, games, cultures and so on. Look at us. Look at us. Look at us. The bad sex headlines are daily, every other day, weekly or so. If we count the headlines that never make social media, the headlines or the news, there are myriads of bad sex headlines every single day. Mixing sex with our games, cultures and agendas produces the tragedy of errors that bombard us with our sex crises.

Queen and King

The sexiest *She* will ever be in this world is Queen. She is perfect. She is perfection. She was created Queen. Woman, you are Queen. Accept no less. Queen is authority. Queen is power. Queen is influence. Queen is image and likeness of God. Queen as in, "You have a domain!" You have spheres of influence. Queen is raising kings: queen is raising queens.

Spirit: mind: soul: heart: body - in her is Queen. Find that. If it is too much to ask to find that in her to love her like that, move on. Queen, if he cannot love you so, be Queen. Your lover is another than him.

The sexiest *He* will ever be in this world is King. Not King over you. But King because he is one with his Super Lover. King with his own scepter, throne and kingdom. A King knows how to love a Queen. He knows who his Queen is.

Spirit: mind: soul: heart: body - in him is King. Queen, if you do not see that when you look at him, look harder or elsewhere. Find that. If it is too much to ask to find that in him to love him like that, move on. King, if she cannot love you so, be King. Your lover is another than her.

When your love reality doesn't match super love, walk, work it, or find someone who will go there with you.

CHAPTER 4
YOUR SEX VIBE

"Evan is a leg man. J.R.? He's all booty. Show me a diva with sexy Double D's, I'll show you Chris." [Lyrics courtesy of *"Triple D, Triple X"*]

We walk around following the feel good.

Killjoy and Prude

Killjoy kills the joy. He literally obliterates anything that may be a source of joy like Scrooge on Holiday. Killjoy cannot fathom that someone finds pleasure in a nice sexy sex thing. The Creator has given us rights to a sex-is-beautiful world (in the context of good). Who are we to force Ms. Sex Killjoy on the populous?

Our sex status quo is hell bent on killing the joy of sex and making a prude out of our sex culture, ourselves and the already impotent. If we could possibly push this "sex is bad" energy like Sahara dust to all eight continents, we would sit back with the sex haters and laugh.

Guess what, people? Sex was designed to be pleasure. It was given to be pleasure. You cannot take that away. Pleasure does not equal the abuses and harassments and injustices. Pleasure in the hands of the wrong person is abused pleasure; it is control; it is less than. It is vital to revisit the pleasure that sex is, but we don't get to contaminate the sex with our bad experiences. Sex is a beautiful thing. If she does not like you looking at her like that, find someone who does. There are millions of women who would love for you to notice them in a good way.

If we can connect with Sex Truth – real Sex Truth - we have a basis to work out our societal sex issues.

Your sex truth is different from his, from hers. Sex has its own truth! It works! It does not make killjoys out of people. It does not make prudish sex cultures with double standards designed to trap the poor bastards. If Sex Truth is boring to you, recalibrate your sex palate. Sex Truth has a vast and diverse landscape of pleasure. Sex cultures have a vast and diverse landscape of pleasures and purposes of their own. If he suffocated to death with your sex cultural norms, recalibrate your sex palate. If you have to bang a monkey to get a high, recalibrate, My Friend. Your thing is your thing, but by the time you get to sexing beasts, you are at the mercy of a beast. The problem is, your next trick could kill you (literally).

We are prone to insatiable if we do not have parameters. When you lose the ability to stop at the last sex high, where do you go from there?

Sex Truth has a freedom that transcends feel good. Master that! Ultimately, we weren't wired to be a slave to anything – not even sexy beautiful sex. If you don't own that – your sex thing - it's your god. It owns you. We're bigger than that.

Le Menage a Mille

No, this is not a fancy layered French dessert. Where have you been? Le menage a trois is all the rage right now. Technically, Le Menage a Trois is French for a household of three (people) but in sex modernity it implies a little more than that. For those of us who are uninformed, it's sexing with three people. Of course, three is a crowd does not apply here and for those who prefer more bodies at once, trois is so boring.

Well, welcome to Le Menage a Trois Culture 101. Brother Man just gunned down his third wheel. You see, he didn't like his Honey doing it with the third wheel.   Of course one might say, "If it ain't for you, don't do it". And, you know what? In our world where superficial sex plays happen ad nauseum, the game for many is just a physical thing (so we say). We just have a fancy word.

Le Menage a Orgy is an old and ancient sex culture. We have nothing on the good old ancients who were sexing in groups like apes and chimpanzees. The bonobo apes – one of our closest animal relatives – are famous for the group sex swing. They were famous for their frequent sex and for sex in lieu of aggression too. Tiberius, a Roman Emperor, loved the orgy. And while some sex cultures say the orgy was practiced by their mythical figures, who did not want to be like the gods? Somehow, transference (or something) has brought the orgy to our Sling and Swing.

So here we are. We're being like the gods with our Les Menages and loving it. Social media now bears (or bares) our tales of last night and we say it loud with pride. No longer are we coding our orgilicious things with hieroglyphics and papyrus paintings. We're on global television and online. We've come a long way but not far at all.

In light of our royal breed, we're still cheating ourselves. Maybe sex was intended to be more frequent; it was intended to be a part of excitement and happiness. Although bodies have changed, I think the designer intended a whole lot more serious sex than our three-week build up to one night a month, once a week, or whatever infrequent sex collection. And maybe, this is why we have Le Menage a Mille (A Household of A Million). By the time Monsieur Le Menage a Mille has done a thousand Les Menages a Quatre across the globe, he's spread his menages to at least a million. Watch out for that Monsieur Menage a Mille. He could be testing positive for everything.

What exactly are you searching for, Friend?

You will not find it there. Love yourself.

Heart Throbbers & 10-Out of-10s

Do you find her beautiful? Before you get to the pussy of her, answer the question: Do you find her beautiful? Why? What is so attractive about her? Why is that so attractive? Describe HER.

What is it about him? Not him – the scandalously heart-throbbing flexer with the six-pack. HIM. What is it about HIM? About man? Do you know man? Do you really know man? Do you know man the image of a super lover? Perhaps, therein lies so much of our maladies. We don't know him – our man. And we don't know the super lover. What does he have to do with sex?

Well, when the super lover who designed sex tells you, "Her love should send you reeling", you should check out the designer. From the Maker of the product, from the manufacturer of sex, comes the directive that you should be reeling from the way she loves you. The maker of sex says, "let her breast satisfy you", "be reeling for her love", "let him kiss me with the kisses of his mouth because your love is better than wine".

Hello Sex Maker!

That's in the manual! Big sexy sex. Big beautiful sex!

When was the last time you were literally reeling from her love?

If she doesn't do that for you, leave her alone.   If you can't send him reeling with the way you love him, leave him alone.

CHAPTER 5
COMMODITIES AND RAW MATERIALS

If you were a king with a kingdom, you'd have rules, laws, protocols and customs. Sex has the same.

We are more superior than just physical. Sex is more superior than physical.

If sex is just a physical experience, you'd be able to get the last boom sex encounter out of your head.   If sex is just a physical phenomenon, you wouldn't have to fight to keep it out of your heart.

We call it sexual abuse; and in some cases, that it is. But, we've abused sex too. If you have to hide to do that - yes, *that* - you're not free. Not privacy: hide. Whatever takes our power to be free to do, owns us – slave. Slave is bigger than chains, bars and San Quentin. Slave is about the mind, the will, the heart. Slave programs us to believe, think and feel a certain way. We are thousands of generations deep in sex slave mentalities that control us sexually and regarding sexuality. We have built societies where we are at fault for the way sex happens. We are building societies where we are at fault for the way sex will play out - in 2022, in 2030, in 3030 - if we don't change. We will build sex societies on a hashtag from 2017 or not.

If we really revisit the original sex blueprint we will see the power
of sex shame. Beautiful sex was free – not free as in zero dollars;
free as in free - no encumbrances, none of our opinions, ways,
unscrupulous gaming manipulations, twisted mindsets, control,
money games, witchiness – just pure beautiful, blissful sex. In the
society of good, we didn't need rules, laws and hashtags. Now,
you can make a few dollars from the sex thing; some are bartering
to own nations using sex games. When you add the ability to make
a few dollars to anything, you have a commodity.

A commodity is a raw material or agricultural product that can be
bought or sold such as aluminum or coffee beans. Notice that the
powers-that-be (not necessarily "the market") determine the price
of gold to be the most valuable - unless we are on the bitcoin ride;
(few can trade here and this ride is still relatively unstable.) The
elite make the rules. Your sex game is a commodity to the players.
Just about everyone is in this particular game: whether we are
playing or not.

The sex trade is bigger than trafficking poor Thai girls or African
minors. The sex trade is sex for career ops, favors with Hollywood
power players, shoving a prostitute in Mr. Senator's face for the
night and your 15-year-old daughter's 25-year-old boyfriend
paying the rent for her booty calls. The list has no end and we are
"sophisticated" with it but we're still trading sex for something.
Where's the line? As long as sex is a commodity, we have a sex
trade and we abuse the sex with our dirty money games. Money
games that could be earning bank as flush as $99 Billion per
annum.

When we take something that was free and bind it in our worlds of
unfair, control-freakish, scheming human systems of play, it loses
its true value – freedom. The thing about sex, resources and

wealth that were created to be free is that they are a power in and of themselves. We cannot enslave them with our games and flippant innuendos and expect for them to abide by our rules. Innately they are free powers. Powers make us pay: not just hashtag payment terms in lawsuits. We lose the power of who we are and good aspects of what the power of sex afforded us. Some of the implications for our sex plays are evident; some we have yet to see; many we cannot bear as a human race.

CHAPTER 6
ON JUDGING

CAVEAT

We all have the right to choose our sex swag free from the biases
of our sex years gone by.
The pain of life is a shaper.
May the pain not leave you crippled.
May the pain not cheat you of your best life.
May we consider deeply what could be if we choose love and
lovers opposite of what our pain dictates.
May we have the courage to choose that.
May we believe that there are still damn good men worth loving
and women who are queens inside.
Even if you are living an exceptional life, is it your best?
What if you could top your greatest life?
How will you ever know if you choose to live from sex pain
biases?

The modern definition of judging is looking down on someone:
treating someone with disapproval: or considering someone
inferior.

The original definition of judging is hearing evidence or legal
arguments (in a case) so that one can pass judgement, decide or

resolve a matter.

We don't have to assume that a masked man who enters our home uninvited and takes our prized 60-inch is a thief. He's a thief. We try to prevent him, call the police, get away from him or all of the above. We confront if we have the audacity because he is doing something wrong. We don't just sit there and watch. Our current sex crisis is not our 60-inch (or 13-inch) and unless we are personally covered deep enough in this crisis to be drowning in it, most of us cannot see that it is more critical than our 60-inch. And, like a thief, we address it.

In addressing the current sex crisis, we are not judging. We are addressing a human crisis that is raping women of their souls: massacring children in sex trafficking: viciously castrating (mostly professionally) men without recourse: obliterating families: empowering institutions and societies to control and execute their unscrupulous agendas: perpetrating greed like white collar crime never could: and etcetera.

Our modern definition of judging is very damning to the poor victim who must sit by and have his 60-inch television stolen and not utter a frown. In so doing, he would be looking down on the thief with contempt. The other definition of judging says, the victim has heard (seen) the evidence that the thief is taking his 60-inch and can make a decision to act in an appropriate way.

Addressing the current sex crisis is addressing the current sex crisis. Here, we are not looking down with contempt on anyone. In addressing our sex crises we hope to (in some way) restore humanity to a level of dignity that is granted to all of us.

Slavery was more than a "nice way" to employ people. It was more than moving nations of people from Africa to the New World to take the slaves' land and their wealth. It cost many of the slaves their lives, physically. Psychologically and emotionally, it cost them their soul. And, today generations of people still fight for their God-given right to be human. They still fight to believe that they are bigger than poverty and handouts. They fight to see that taking their brothers' lives is not a normal that anyone should accept.

The dehumanizing of any person is dawg. When you take man out of him, you're a thief. When you take woman out of her that is criminal. You cannot take a human being's soul and expect for them to be human. That is a part of what separates us from animal. For years women have been dehumanized by the sex crisis. Many men have been stripped of their Man in our current sex war: many of them falsely accused. It is imperative that we address it. How we address the sex crisis determines whether we survive this or take centuries of steps back.

In addressing our sex crises, we are saying (in many cases), "We are doing something wrong". We are saying so that we can address it appropriately. We're not condemning, looking down on, nor judging. We're telling us to stop doing what is wrong and detrimental. That is wrong! Put the television back or suffer the consequences. Address this sex crime issue in the right way or suffer the consequences.

We're not telling you you're doing something wrong because we're perfect. What YOU are doing is not about our perfect nor our flaws. Don't make it about our imperfections and flaws to take the attention off what you are doing wrong. It is critical that we all face ourselves.

We live in a world where we do not, under any circumstances, face ourselves. "SHADE" is a dagger and we don't get to "throw shade" no matter how much it may save a life or a generation. No, we're not looking down on you by saying, "Fix that". Just like a parent who tells their child to fix that is not looking down on them. Mama loves you enough to tell you, "That will kill you!" What Mama tells you won't kill you. THAT will kill you. Face your THAT and walk away from the killer. Love your Mama.

Our modernity would daresay the victim of the 60-inch thief invited bad karma on himself because he did something wrong and so the thief is justified in what he did. When we waver in places of sometimes right is right, we rob ourselves of justice. A thief is a thief. Bad sex is bad sex.

Where do we get our consciences on sex, sexual practices and injustices? Where did our 2017 sex conscience tsunami come from? The 2016 elections? The politicking behind the scenes that spread like propaganda? Or, the hashtags that serve the power players behind the scenes (inadvertently or intentionally)?

How do we suddenly insist on enforcing our laws on an agenda thousands of years old, steeped in the genetic code of a human race and as prevalent as dirt? What is behind our sudden onslaught of sex etiquette? We have sex killer storms that destroy families and people's lives; and, we walk on as if nothing happened. What is behind it? Who sets the price and what is the market? Why are they setting the price and calling shots all of a sudden? Is your sex thing more valuable that his or hers? Why? Because you screwed a top gun? Or is it because you have bank? What about Sex Slave over there who got screwed by a small fry?

CHAPTER 7
GUILT

Many sexual crises are covered up in the sexual issues of the past that most of the generations before carried to their grave. Many of our current sexual issues stem from the sex cover ups from *them*. The limelight is on our sex places and we are expected to dance but don't really know the tune.

They expect the sexually marred to tell a story they only know in part. They don't know that the lyrics come from their parents, their grandparents, their great grandparents and thousands of years before. Above-the-law systems and institutions, rash hashtags and sexual justice radicals don't know nor care that there is no platform to tell *that* story. It doesn't matter that victims and perpetrators of sex places were not there for their parents, grandparents and great grandparents sex places; they are expected to carry their load. 2018 learned their sex culture from back there. The sex crises have evolved into gamuts of sex and sexuality with personalities that may look different from the ancient sex plays, but the roots are the same. If we are here today, it is astounding where they will be tomorrow if we don't make a steep turn in a different sex direction now.

This year is genetically coded with the sex deviances from back there. Who cares? Today is expected to pay. You are responsible for what you do sexually, 2018! You are responsible, 2050 and 4050! They don't care about your damn sex DNA and genetic code that molests young boys, girls and/or animals. You must pay! If our sex revolution only demands payment without going there, the sex degenerate stays intact and morphs into a more atrociously deadly power.

"The past is the past; leave the past. Let's just make 'em pay and move on."

We've been moving on. The pasts we left behind are killing people. Tomorrow our daughters and sons will be on the line because we did not fix the problem; they are already on the line. We cannot fix the problem by demanding payment alone.

If this is really about equality and rights and sexual good, we have to recode the "bastards" learning to be bastards or predisposed to be bastards because their mother, their father and their generations were bastards. If you learn to be nice, you will be nice (most likely). If you learn to be a bastard or a bitch, most likely, you will be a bastard or a bitch. (Deep down inside, none of us are bastards nor bitches – some of us have learned to be.)

The world is rampant with nice people and people who act like bastards and bitches. Clean up the bastards and bitches at the core. If all we're doing is paying money to be bastards and bitches for bad sex games, we may as well set the fines on bad sexing like damn parking tickets. We've still not changed the learned core of a human being. Nobody's interested in changing the faux core of anyone. Faux core: who we think we are. Core: who we really are – image of God.

The sex hell is very real for those who live in it. Children get raped every day in our world. Few, if any, are interested in that enough to go to the core, dig up the roots and kill them; because we are after one bastard we hate or the one who is paying us. While we're busy trying to take one "bastard" down, another child just got sold into sex slavery.

Guilt has a way about it. It loves to deflect blame to everything else. It has yet to say, this is my fault or that was my fault. It will do everything to make it everyone else's fault. And, many times there is someone else to blame.

Guilt is a control freak that keeps us in condemnation of ourselves, them and our pasts. Guilt is a good indicator that something went wrong. Guilt tells us we still have humanity enough to feel. What we do with our feelings determines if we heal, become better, go bitter or rot to our core to the point of no return. It is apparent that some of us are not healing well. We can heal only as far as we go. If we embrace healing, there are no limits to where we can go. Guilt has us rely on our own strength to carry loads we are not built to bear.

It is okay to say, "I'm sorry" (whether it is enough or not). It is unnecessary to live guilty or to die guilty. A perpetrator may never say, "I'm sorry". A victim may never say, "You killed me inside". They may never accept his apology. But, it is okay to say ... something. It is okay to say something to someone worthy of hearing what you have to say. When you say, it is no longer hidden. It loses its power to hold you. You make significant steps to get your freedom. How we say what we say is critical. Why we say what we say tells a good story or a detrimental one. Why we say perpetuates the darkness, gives the darkness power or makes light stronger. *When* we say may be more beneficial now than then. If we say, is up to us. If we say to the wrong people, it can be more harmful.

It is not so much that we want equality and fairness. We are fighting for something that we have. The sexually abused have proven they don't need the system to make it. We are gifted - all of us - with what it takes to make it (to somewhere) in our societies. We're not talking about making it, though. It is success that we speak of: success that transcends money and class: success that is truly free.

Ultimately, we will always seek a savior. For most of us, our SEEK is so subconscious, we deny that we need a savior. Our mama can't bear that. We try out all sorts of things and people because deep within, the human chasm has this irresistible need to be saved. Even if we "Get Jesus", he "fails" us. Why? Because Jesus ain' saving us our way. Our way? Sex ourselves to death until we draw our last breath: highs that melt the cartilage in our nostrils: selfish-mess that owns the world. Really. The human soul is that insatiable. You better own that somehow or it will kill you. That greedy little "id" in us we call soul will drive us to death. What to do? Find something worthy and do it with your passion. What else to do? Own your "id"? What else to do?

CHAPTER 8
WHY WE SAY

There is an indescribable power in a woman who can sit at a roundtable of such volatile issues and discuss her sexual victimization with a level of civility that can be trusted. Real power, men, is the ability to listen to a subordinate or a woman to hear, to understand and to educate yourself to be an effective change agent in this sex crisis. Real power is facing your sex stories and being honest about them in good environments. Real power is helping your brother out. Real power, men, is standing up, respectfully, for yourself when you need to. Real power is ...

Every woman cannot say without screaming dagger words, emotions and intentions. That is understandable: even respected. It's just harder to pay attention. Even when someone hears the sound of screaming words, the daggers frighten them from coming to the table to listen and do.

One of the reasons why we say is a part of being successful at humanity. A part of being successful at humanity is having that - a safe place to go. We should ask that. Why didn't the molested, the sexually harassed and assaulted, the rape victim, have a safe place to go? We all need that – safe places to go. Safe places are a part of one of our basic instincts – survival.

A part of the silence is that – there is no place to go where someone trying to help a victim can bear their load. The circles of good humanity get broken with sexual injustices and corruption. That is another reason why we say. We say because societies are still passive instead of proactive in *preventing*. We say because the money does not change victims; it does not unrape her. Money does not heal the abused inside. If at all possible, it is necessary to prevent. The atrocities leave marks that never heal for many victims.

We say because it hurts. We say because it costs too much. The pain is excruciating for the residuals of sex corruption. The price is too high. For some, it costs a normal life; for others, the price is years of darkness or depression. For some, it costs everything.

A nine-year-old girl, Huriya, died from rape in the Middle East. Huriya is not the only one. We say, because we cannot sit silently by and know that another child is in a closet somewhere today. We say because Mommy has to be aware. Daddy needs to know. If you don't care enough to be there for your children (somehow), find someone who can or forego having them. If you don't want them, find someone who does. The world is a beautiful place; it is a toxic place. And, sometimes, it is a deadly place. If you will not spend yourself giving your children (your child) a life that makes this a beautiful place for them, it is unfair that they live anything less. We cannot exhaust love. Wealth like this is a superfluous-sustainable resource. (Superfluous-sustainable: from an infinitely abundant source). If there were 20 billion more children and twice as many of us, there would still be a world of love untapped and quadrillions of dollars in wealth to spend. Human is limited. Love and wealth like this are not.

We say because regimes and governments, authorities and

persuasions continue practices that cost children their lives. We applaud the one out of one million that makes it from the ashes. We have a responsibility to the 999,999. Where are your children? Where are your children right now? Right this minute, where are your children? Nations, where are your children? Where is the money that has passed through your hands for them to make their lives better? Where is the money? Where are their resources? Why did you steal from them? Why are they less than the filthy gravel beneath your feet? Why do you not care?

We say because we need to care! We say because we need to care enough to change it! We say because we need to fix it! Right now! We have within our power to fix it and change it and to do. Leaders have within their power to fix it, change it and to do; most of them refuse to fix, change, and eliminate sex corruption and abuses. You are as guilty as the perpetrators, as the rapists, as the abusers if you don't fix it, change it, and facilitate healing.

Victims and women need to be validated. The truth needs to be and the lies need to be exposed in environments that are fair. Exposing lies can be as deadly as keeping them inside. People's lives are at stake. The broken systems don't allow for etiquette with such improprieties; sometimes there are no established systems and protocols for exposing lies and "kill the bastard" methodologies.

> Kill the bastard(s) or KTB: destroying an *alleged* sex perpetrator's (or a sex perpetrator's) life, career or future by attacking them: many times without due course: many times with poisonous vengeful hate: many times with malicious lies and witchy intent: especially publicly.

Know what you're doing when you say, why you're doing and

how you're doing. Does it help the victim heal? Is it directed to the perpetrator to help them, bring them to understanding or justice, stop them or heal them? We don't have to empathize with perpetrators but most of them have sex issues as deep as yours or deeper. If we can find the destructive roots and destroy them, we are most effective. If we are spreading more hatred and evil by dirty motives in saying, we become as they are.

CHAPTER 9
UNDERHANDED

Connive: /ke' niv/. Secretly allow (something considered immoral, illegal, wrong or harmful) to occur. Secretly do something considered immoral, illegal, wrong or harmful.

Connive means you knew what you were (are) doing. Again we are operating in a realm outside of the good box. If you're doing him for pleasure or fun and secretly (secretly) taping the sexcapade to use against him, you are not doing him for pleasure nor for fun. If your sex man (target) is that unscrupulous (especially, if you know it), why are you sexing him?

Blackmail. Blackmail. Blackmail.

Ms. Money, why are you doing someone so far Deep South (scruple-less)?

Climbing the Ladder

Inherently, women have been made to feel that they don't count. In part, some of us do the sex and attraction thing because we feel that is how to play in order to advance. Some of us have been taught (explicitly or implicitly) that is how to play.

We are valuable because we exist, not because we have a gold globe in our corner office or lead the epics on the big screen. Ahhh! Fundamentally, that is in part why we stay (at sexually-harassed jobs). It's not about just the money and the job. We stay because we value our-SELF by what THEY say, by what THEY think about us, by how THEY treat us. We value our-SELF by what we do. We are driven by public opinion and fame in the air. We are driven by what we grew up with. We are driven by how they treat us; how they treated our mother; what they did to our father: and so on. Women, you are valuable because you are! YOU need to believe that! We need to believe that.

When you attend the boss' hotel suite on the business trip, you just tripped your-SELF up.

Why are you in his suite?

You: He's the boss and insisted that we meet in his suite.

Call his superior? Suggest a work setting with witnesses (people) around. If it's after hours and he insists on meeting up, go somewhere public and safe.

You (yelling flames): He insisted that I meet at his hotel suite!

What happens next? It's one thing to go to the boss' hotel suite or the colleague's house. It's another to have a dirty Manhattan Martini. It's quite another to have one with lustful R&B or smooth smooth jazz in the air. It's quite another to take a pill "to help you relax". What are you relaxing for? It's work. Know when to go home. Report his ass on the way to the elevator or cab or car. Dignity is more valuable than 9-to-5 money or $1M in hush-bucks.

It's okay for women to make some of The Rules but where are we coming from? We cannot be biased in our stance or bitter in our hearts and make fair rules. Let women speak their stories, but some of us must ask some questions of our hearts if we want to address the sex crises comprehensively; we must ask questions of our-SELF. Why do you give him your number after he sexually assaults or harasses you? Why are you still working at his job? It is unconscionable for sex favors and innuendos to be a "requirement" to have his filthy job. Women, you are better than that. As unspoken or un-said as it is, if you have to do that to keep your job, it is a job requirement. Read your actual job requirement.

This element of fear that women have of losing their jobs or staying at the foot of the corporate ladder is slavery. AGAIN: You are better than that. It is okay to launch a winner job search for employment where you are respected or summon the gifts and talents inside yourself and kick ass. You can do it! Work and pay your bills, but you are more valuable than inflating the ego of a jackass. A power player is trained to know that everybody wants something from him/her. Most of them take advantage of that.

There are millions of good men and women to work for where you get to keep your dignity.

The Set Up

Men, watch for women coming back (willingly) for more.

Control your things, BRUH! She's wired! More wired than an FBI/Italian mafia spy game. And these days, wired means satellites, invisible drones, spyware and GPS in orbits that you will never find in her bra. One woman admitted to going back wired. Come on, Women! Cut the "innocence" game if you are playing dirty. Women know what they are doing. Most of them knew what they were doing back then.

With our myriad of sexual crime cases, when is it vital and fair to consider malicious intent by some women? Especially, when women wait until he's famous, prime minister or one of the good ol' boys. When are we trying to get justice and when are we trying to destroy someone? Not because of a wrong they did but because he "made it", or because he picked her instead of me, or because ...

Sexual crimes are illegal and wrong. That is a principle whether he is just the manager or if he is the power player. That is a principle whether the legal system will fail us or not. If they don't believe us or we get fired for speaking up, sexual crimes are illegal and wrong. If it was illegal when he was the manager, why wasn't it reported and justice executed?

When we wait to report sex crimes because he's gone mogul, what exactly is our intent? It looks really malicious. It looks like a resentful, spiteful streak hit us that "the bastard" who did this is arriving (somewhere) and nobody knows what he did. There is something about him getting away with it. Reporting him because he got away with it is a different motivation than reporting him because what he did was wrong and illegal. What he did is as appalling during his mogul tenure as it was when he was a manager, a mail attendant or poor. Sexual crimes have no class distinction, race discrimination, nor professional grade. They are sexual crimes. Check your heart if it is okay for the mogul to sexually harass you but not the garbage collector. Why blow off the poor cashier who sexually harassed you and go after the filthy rich power player? It just looks like it's about money when it's about the principle; sex crimes are wrong no matter who the perpetrator is: rich, poor, beggar, thief. Check your heart if it is okay for The Hottie to sexually assault you but not Average Man.

Women, we don't decide if the systems will treat us fairly but we have a right – at the time – to report illegal sexual behavior.

Women, watch out for wanting favors from Mr. Boss and Mr. Power Player.

What do you have to pay for that corner office?   The bitch of it is, when you arrive, you can't even sit down for batting flies. What do you have to give for that role on the big screen? (If that is what you are doing.) If you have to sex to get that, you will have to sex more to keep it. There's another sexy Sexy who will sex more than you to get that. Games. Then the loser gets mad and cries, "Sexual Harassment", "Sexual Assault", "Rape", "Grope", or one of our sexual crime accusations.

Women, if you're specifically *sexing* to get that, you have no right to accuse him of sexual harassment or sexual whatever. You gave him some to get something. If you don't get what you traded your things for, you lost that one. It was a game when you started trading (technically, prostitution). You cannot play games with your sex, be a sore loser, then join the women who are really victimized and ruin their cause. You were playing a game. They were taken advantage of. If you were gaming with his sexual favors and didn't get the prize, he has a right to say, "that was about the prize" if you decide to make sexual crimes claims.

Prostitution: to engage in any sexual act, sexual contract or unacceptable sexual intercourse for something of value or for money.

There are laws against prostitution.

Sexual justice advocates and victims, don't let the gamers in on your causes and hashtags unless they come clean. Their dirty motives rot your foundation.

CHAPTER 10
THE CONTRACT

Sex File

She knew by the way he looked at her that she was his sex pick of the night. She was waiting for him too. He asked …

She said: For what?
He said: I will give you killer bank.
She said: Sign here.

Sign here, but I want your power, your wealth, your life. [Gimme your echelon society ring, your Rolex and your kingdom – i.e. your authority, your soul, your life. In other words, "I own you, Bitch!"]

He signed.

He was desperate for a piece of ass, but he must have known how he would get his life back. He did send her killer bank. Well, he sent his BFF to give her the killer bank and to get his stuff back. The problem is, she wasn't there. His authority, his soul and his life were not nearly as important as the child she was carrying for him. For him, this was not a part of the contract. For her? It was everything. She was carrying his seed. What more proof did she need? What was more valuable to him than seed?

Getting yourself pregnant with his child in order to own a piece of his ass, collect alimony checks, take his things and etcetera-etcetera is such an old story. We've mastered this (to some extent). It is deliberate, intentional and culture for many women. It infests so many cultures globally, it's Woman Culture (for many women). The Sex Contract is just a part of big business these days. Here goes.

Man, you are royalty. What are you doing selling your kingdom for ass? For some reason – with all of the gender wars – men and women still think the no-strings-attached aspect of relationships like these is ideal.

Man: She has my baby so that I can leave seed.

Woman: He gives me money [like a Baby Daddy] to have his children so I can buy anything I want.

The shit that has resulted from these arrangements is so shitty, he wishes he had died childless like a seedless GMO globe grape. Get yourself a real thing, Man. Woman, get a job and if you really want a family, be all that – family worthy. If all you're doing is pumping babies out for money, you don't want your children. Eventually, many of them become a "burden to society". Oh, correction here. You want them to the extent that they bring in some money – from their Big Daddy Cash or when they get a job.

In the saga of our Sex File, this Baby Daddy was the leader of an entire nation, prince of a kingdom, heir to royalty. Yet, he would leave all of that in the hands of her: a woman playing prostitute. Why? For him it was a one night stand. He didn't know the players behind his scene who were after his all. For this faux prostitute, she knew the game. She made a deal.

What was the deal? The deal was a contract – a sex contract. She went for the kill. He was so desperate for a swig o' pussy, he signed her contract. Then, he thought he could get away with it. He didn't care that he left everything there, with a "fake prostitute". He just wanted the sex thing bad: that bad. He underestimated her; after all, *she* was just a prostitute; after all she was just a woman. Men, don't underestimate the masters of The "With Child" Game; don't be so desperate to leave your mark that you sell your all to someone who will take your all. Find a good queen worthy of your seed if you want a child that badly. Everyone is not worthy of your seed.

She said: "Here's the deal." [She's already calling the shots.] "You have a swig o' ass but I own you."

We call it Gold Digging. The dictionaries define it as forming a relationship with someone to get money or presents/gifts from them. People aren't digging. Digging requires exertion of extreme effort, skill and strategy. Flaunting a pussy is a pastime for many and Mr. Player isn't even trying to avoid the pussies flying around in his face.

The pussy is the lure; the prize is his money.

If you will sex her, you will sell out or eventually you will sellout (if you're not already SOLD!). Women flaunt their pussies in men's faces every day hoping to buy a life of trinkets, financial security, a phone card or just to have. Then they sell their prey (our current Sex War Mr. Bastard) to the highest bidder. There are men who do the same.

Some things are given to us. When we stay in the chains of bad sex places we give up our sexy sex to whoever stole it or took it from us. A fake prostitute, though?

CHAPTER 11
MAN, MAN, MAN, MAN, MAN

Surely you can control your libido better than that. You are royalty. You are god. You make your own rules not bow to other gods. C'mon Man! Man up!

Women are going public because it is one way to get men addressed. Why is there a lack of intervention in the male community with accountability that confronts his peer, his brother, his friend?

Hey, my brother, "Get in line."

Hey, my brother, "What happened here?"

Hey, my brother, "You need to fix that!"

("That" being the inclination to sexual misconduct, sexual harassment, sexual crime: his marred soul.)

More powerful than that urge to sex splurge and more dramatic than the lure of your sex soiree, is the masterplan behind it all. The sex big picture is always in play. Before we graced the stage of our human affairs, the sex big picture was in play. It was all good until another agenda entered the stage of human affairs. The other agenda is the grand stratagem to destroy: humanity and anything good.

It is futility to argue the nonexistence of evil any more. It used to be that such bad things happened in that country or over there. When gunmen kill seventeen, one, fifty or two in fits of rage psychology has yet to classify, it is obvious that all is not good. When officials arrest 80 for sex trafficking in the U.S. and rescue hundreds of teenage girls in the United States from sex offenders, all is not good.

Many of us are playing king-pin status in the dirty sex game and saying we don't believe that evil forces exist. That is not surprising. The evidence is all around. Of course we don't believe. Mr. Sexual Misconduct just got fired; Ms. Fling just cashed her check from her winnings in her sexual misconduct lawsuit. By the way, Mr. Sexual Misconduct only said "Hello Beautiful" to her. On another note, Mr. First Degree Rape has to serve his maximum sentence while his wife struggles to provide for their four minor children. His victim cannot find her soul.

Normal civilized peoples can govern themselves to society's norms. Habitual sexers can try to break the habit or control themselves. Trained sexers – whether by early sexual abuse or other sex exposure – can live in the game. They still have a force greater than themselves to contend with: they have been exposed to the other side. The sex demoniac cannot help themselves. They play sex games with the devil and they love it. The rest of the normal people who have not been trained to sex from the age of three, four, childhood or adolescence *may* develop healthy sex lives; some of the abused do too.

A part of society's problem is we insist on applying laws of humanity to what is non-human. Folks, you cannot treat the devil with human laws. He is not from here. If Mr. Sex Offender or

Mrs. Sex Player has crossed the line of human into other, consider what is behind the sex play.

Why is she taping their sex game to take him down later?

That is conniving – civil and good does not play like that.

That is fear – with fear in the equation, anything is possible.

Your sex diva is a thief. When she threatens to roll the tape and states her price to keep her mouth shut, you have to go to the bank, Man. There are ways to roll the tape within the parameters of our sex laws. Perhaps, she doesn't care what she has to lose. You may have more to lose that she does. She will keep threatening to roll the tape. You have to keep going to the bank. When you're tired paying, you are going down. Check mate! Queen trumps king pin. You're a pawn, Bro. This is how the kingdom of darkness plays.

The Other Side of the Stories

They wait in sleazy lingerie for young professionals on the first rung of the career ladder. Grown women, trained in Sex Roulette, bait the young and innocent or the big wig to position themselves in money games of the rich and society. They play for their own bank or gain: old story. The old stories are now entertainment - watch TV; read the Online Headlines; browse social media posts.

The sex stories are everywhere. Some of them are abuse stories, some are sex games. Women and men are playing. The agendas call out the dog they are trying to destroy and let the other player go free; some go free until their sex crimes are needed for ammo. Again, nobody is asking the questions about Queen Sexy's audacity to sex a married man. No one is holding her to the protocols of society. A minor percentage is into the fact that his wife is home with their children. As a matter of fact, Queen Sexy knows when to go for the prey. She knows his wife is on overload and she knows that his wife is not sexing him. Oh, Honey (distracted or busy wife), they love you! They see you coming! Queen Sexy positions herself to be there. Yes, wherever the Bastard Husband is, she's there.

Poor Wifey. Queen Sexy couldn't give a rat's whisker about wifey. You know what, Bastard Husband? Queen Sexy is just doing her job. Do yours. Be a husband. No, not the man. Be a husband. You can have a thousand men and never have a husband. Wedding bands don't make him a husband and her a wife. BE. Be what and who you are. You don't just change from being a man to a husband. As much as it may be in you to be Husband, you still have to be that. It is in you to be a husband.

Parents must train boys to be that. Parents must train girls to be wives. Not subservient slaves: wives. We have societies that still have no idea that just because you got married, you're not a husband and a wife. King Priest can pronounce you husband and wife until the next wedding bell vibrates the cathedral. You cannot pronounce a man a husband and a woman a wife. Husband is soul, mind, body and spirit in every sense of the word husband. Wife is the same. Hello divorce or hello sweet longevity? What is a husband? What is a wife?

I know, I know. We're not into that – sweet longevity. We like the Hollywood version of Longevity and Nuptials. Your children are dying because the meagre foundation they had is destroyed.   If we don't get into it, we will pay more than what we can afford. People already are (paying). The pain is lovely to your hater. Your hater takes pain and makes bitter poison. You have the choice to take pain and make glory.

Sexing Kings

The Queen of Hearts owns the king of hearts, the king of spades, the king of diamonds, king of clubs and kingpin. In *Ways of a Queen*, Jez was always on top.

Jez means satan is your husband: Jez is loyal to satan.

With whips and chains, she dominates.

CAVEAT: Every Whip and Chain thing is not a domination thing.

This one is. Jez' man is down. He's not just pussy-whipped. He's whipped.

Where's the man? Where are the men? When you lay yourself down to be whipped by *her* for a piece of ass, Bad Boy, where's the man? Who's the man? Don't lose your man for a piece of ass. This isn't about whips and chains as much as it is about letting a woman WITH A DAWG MOTIVE whip your ass. If someone loves you and that's how you play, play, play, play. But Mr. Whippy Chains, if she's the average load-toting diva with baggage, you're at the mercy of a witch for a piece of ass.

You cannot sex Jez, O King, and think you have leverage. Girlfriend belongs to satan. (Of course, satan is too far-fetched for so many of us, but we cannot explain our ways, our sex crises, our devious). Jez has no allegiance to you, no matter what your covenants. She can only take *from* you. You get nothing in return. It may look like you got a bone. That's to add to the rest of the bones in your sack so that when Winner Takes All is over, she has your sack of bones, your things and your soul. Checkmate, O King! You lose! Again. You cannot win.

There are leaders who don't play with Jez. The ones who play Jez' games to get their own booty, she owns most of them. Jez owns. Leaders who don't play Jez' games own their game. Oh, Jez does have something the king players who sit out her game wants.

Some of them are too scared to play to get it. Others strategize to get what they want without her. Some will take her out of the equation. The wisest kings know that Jez really does not own anything. They know the source of her booty. They just go to the source and get it.

CHAPTER 12
THE SCANDAL SHOW

If our world was just cut and dried, we could assume any show is
what it is. Don't take every big show at face value. If you see a
big fish going down, trace the line or the trajectory of the spear that
took him out. Dig a little deeper. There are bigger fish to fry and
agendas to accomplish; and, if you sniff the air, you will find the
scent of stink money. Oh, money is sweet, but like the sex, we
have mastered the art of contaminating it.

Roll the Tape: The Sex Tape

Two can play this game, so if you think you want to play "Roll the
Sex Tape", know your game. After all, there are at least two of
you on the tape. Unless you're selling porn, why do you have a
sex tape? How does it benefit the wider population? They can't
use it for Sex Ed like that. Some of our kids know more than us.

No matter how well you play The Sex Game, someone always
plays better than you. Even the maestro loses: sometimes
eventually.

The Rules? You don't have a fair playing field playing with your
own rules that don't fly in the big game. While you're making

rules to win your "local" game, the big leaguers have rules of their own. What you got, Beautiful?

If the cameras give you some kind of high, Buddy, let go and jump: preferably with a parachute.

Why are you showing up to a sex scene like a cinematographer for the next big screen hit or a camera tech with hidden devices?

The fact that we need a bill to address the Sex Tape says, it's a problem. Revenge porn is a problem for victims and perpetrators. For the power players who don't want their sex plays public, anti-revenge porn laws could be sweet relief. Unfortunately, for the one holding the sex tape over his head - Mr. Sextortion or Ms. Sextortion – anti-revenge porn laws could affect her game. Of course, Mr. Sextortion or Ms. Sextortion can use their tapes in other ways.

If you thought you had a way to control your sex player in the sex game, think twice with revenge porn laws. You may be the one paying, Ms. Sextortion.

If he's sexing you with the cameras rolling, most likely your sex thing is about negative "energy" [bad spirit]. Anything you say or do can be used against you on social media, in The Control Game, The Money Game, The Sex Game and every other game.

#1 You can't even enjoy yourself.

If you have to stash evidence on your sex liaison, what is that? You can't trust him?

#2 Find somebody trustworthy.

How boring! Trust issues leave us leery in revenge porn games. Well, we have a lot of issues, but the trust issues are very expensive. Think about the stakes before you roll with sexies who have trust issues. The best of relationships have come to this – sex footage, just in case. If you must go that low, what do you really have?

Get a job if you're recording footage of your sex place to slay someone for money. You're a criminal. You may escape the law or even use your footage with the law, but life comes back around. Life bites back hard on the vengeful.

The Intent

If you are sexing someone and you need a stage, action, lights and Take 14, what are you doing? If you can trust her to take sex footage of you today, what about tomorrow? Relationships have a way of going South: Deep South. Even for the best of them, the well-intentioned and the faithful ones, sometimes IT happens.

If he is hiding the camera, you've got trouble, Honey! Vice-versa! Depending on how high you're going, Mr. Power Player, the stakes are even higher to have your ass in a very compromising position for your beautiful world to see. Keep your ass off the camera!

Everyone is not sex gaming.

Some of the people who come out (or roll the tape in public), come out for noble reasons. For the victim who beats the darkness to rise every day, fighting the darkness gets old. Just because you come out, does not mean you have to come out on the world stage. The goal is liberating yourself. Sometimes, the only way out is on the world stage because sex power players have become impossible formidable entities.

CHAPTER 13
THE BIG SEX AGENDA

Who's getting paid? Some SOME *SOME* of the divas are getting paid, were hired to take him down, or are being paid to crash men. Take a step back if you love the sex (game) too much or more than your soul. Who sent her? Who sent him? Is it just innocent attraction? Is it not? The conniving put a totally different spin on the way we look at sex. If sex is your dope, Buddy, you'd better have a vice to save you that is bigger than that. Sex attraction is really money attraction sometimes. For her, money may be bank; for her, a joint; for her, position; for her, an acting role.

If she's attracted to money like that, sex may be her ways-and-means committee. If he's attracted to sex, money may be his ways-and-means committee. Big Money equals Big Attraction: Big Sex equals Big Attraction. It does not matter your physique, your religion, your looks. Big Money and Big Sex have this way of making satan look nice.

Many times we seek retribution for what he did to us in bankrupt places. The system is designed to "make 'em pay"; and in some cases, payment is exacted. Money has its place, but it has yet to fix the life, the heart, our humanity; it cannot make us whole. The money doesn't heal you; money cannot heal our world. It may make life better or feel like justice was served, but the gaping chasms of emotional devastation still eat away. Sometimes it gets better with time and we learn to cope or get over, but whole? Not with just money.

Whole is not a figment. It is possible. It is foundational to healthy relationships. Whole is where we rise to living big picture status. Everything else is vile in comparison. Go for whole... Even the wealthiest can live soul bankrupt. He was a king but sex desperate enough for a night with a pretend prostitute. He was the leader of one of the greatest nations on earth but killed a man to cover up adultery with the man's wife. Welcome to our world now.

Today's Headlines

His greatest successes and biggest bank could not heal his soul. He died in a prison cell. His associates were The Prominent – leaders, the wealthy and royalty. His associates play all the right cards to keep the eyes of the world on him where he lies dead in a prison cell.

He was a wealthy Who's Who in the international sex trafficking market. His personal rolodex has the names of world leaders and power players but no one is talking about that. Comprehensively, we need to talk about things like that if we really want to kill a sex crisis. If we go there, we get behind the sex scene to what is happening in the control towers of our sex affairs. So far, we're just puppets on a stage of sex wars and that is unfair to the bastards going down when those at the controls are guilty too: some more guilty than the "bastard" they shove into the limelight.

The power players in the dirty game have directed the media to play out the saga of their dead associate's wealth, his will, his exes and his children: who may be his children or not. Playing his dirty life story for our sensationalism takes the heat off them and instead obliterates their dead friend. At the end of the day, the societies and systems of power players typically sell out someone to save themselves; they have done that before and will continue unless all of the cards are played. Power players sell out the Bastard of the Day to jockey for position in their societies and to take down leaders so that they own nations, economies and the bank. There is no "The END" here if we continue the sex games. What is your story worth?

The human chasm is too deep and ever widening. We have these damn insatiable chasms just because we're human – mo' money, mo' power, mo' sex, mo' dope, mo' fame, mo' salacity, mo' stories, mo' cults, mo' melodramatic drama, mo'... Bigger and better is a part of who we are. How we get there and what's behind the greed and insatiables can be the death of us.

There will always be another power player and a bigger game. The "beauty" of what we see in the media with Ms. Money and Mr. Sex is, it is a showcase of the bigger games that we cannot see – Stock Market size games, World Market size games, power struggles among nations. The Cold War is melting the arctic. If you could see the economic games behind the scenes, the sex plays would fall into place.

Ms. Money's game really is bigger. If they can take down the power player that she is screwing (was screwing), they have leverage in their own foul game again. You see, Ms. Money and her Power Player are bigger than Sex Barter. Sex Barter is just the hook. The big fish are at the end of the line. And, this is not fishing for Wahoo. The stakes are high in the game. Watch the world's markets, trade and economies.

Insecurity was always there for the power players: for us. For power players, insecurity about who owns the power, the wealth, the plays. Insecurity intimates a need for security; the price is too high sometimes but we pay anyway. Arrogance was always there. Arrogance is not arrogance until we cross the lines. What was denied or just missing in our little boy places turns into demon places if we let them. Humble beginnings don't always equal humble power. Power has a tendency to go to our heads. Succeed but, stay humble: keep loving people: have an unshakeable core rooted in good.

One of the most blatant pictures that our Sex World paints is humanity's natural gift to abuse (anything). We are naturally, not innately, inclined to destruction unless we live from the higher instinct that we all have to live well. We abuse power, annihilate beauty, kill truth and live mediocre.

Inside you are king. Inside you are queen. The big stage is vicious – the fierce war of the big stage is just Game. Graceful will sometimes allow the pitfalls to flesh us out to who we really are inside – unfathomable greatness. The big stage of Game loves dirty melodramatic stories that go viral and take down kings and queens. Watch who you pledge your allegiance to – Graceful or Game.

CHAPTER 14
CONTROL: TIME'S UP

We call it Women's Rights, Victim's Rights, Sexual Justice, Et Al, but, for the most part, many people are using sexual justice movements as destroyers. The malicious intent to destroy a human being and promote oneself on that premise makes the farce a destroyer. Of course, harassment is wrong. That is fundamental and basic. We are beyond right and wrong. Sexual crime is at the core of our cause.

Sexual crime: sexual misconduct, sexual harassment, sexual bad, sexual abuse, sex trafficking, rape, every world of sex deviance.

It is one thing to reprimand perpetrators, address the systems and the laws, change things, or fix our sex-related issues. It is another to bulldoze, annihilate and destroy everything in our path on the way to ...

Where do we think we're going? News flash: You cannot build greatness on that. You don't build great systems, great politics, great institutions, great relationships, great marriages, great families, great nations on rubbles of hatred, injustice and evil. The foundation is bad. It [whatever we think we're building] will crumble. That's just basic.

Don't lose your beauty to the hate. Beauty is more than botox-plump red lips and thigh gaps. Beauty is true beauty inside and out: in every sense of the word beauty. We have yet to tap who and what we are. Woman qualifies us to be queen, beautiful, sexy and to love.

We lose who we are in the lust for power the wrong way. Our power is our own - inalienable. We give it away when we are bad haters, when we trade our precious for... Hating evil is good but work it out. When the method is counterproductive to the goal, our weapons (sexual justice, equality, feminism) become toxic suicide. Yes, you may take a few down with you, but the demons live on.

We live in an era where we're not that sacrificing for the next generation so who cares if they live or die because we lost the cause on pathetic methodologies? One of the worst things about demons is they have a way of morphing into more deadly killers. Some of us don't care that much about our children to care if we create deadlier demons with our fight. If our children aren't that important, the demons will find a way to slay something we love so deeply, it's in our core; it is connected to our life. Hold your precious tightly. What is your precious?

Divas, you can only play men for their money for so long. Many men are starting to cheat on you ON PURPOSE. That money game you're playing to make sure he has a good steady job before you even date him to confirm the bank is there for your kill, Honey? He knows how to take blades to your soul. He will cheat on you until your soul bleeds. It's not so much that men may be cheating more than ever. Now, the cheat is sweet payback. And, they love it! It's intentional, Queen. The cheat is to kill your core, Queen.

Men will continue to do it, if we continue to challenge them with our ill-will sex wars. (All sex wars are not ill-will.) Many men are just warming up to the Two-Can-Play-This-Game game. Women are declaring war on men and expect no retaliation. Every man is not going to roll over to your sweet ass and play dead. If you think you know how to go for the kill by taking him for what he has, watch your back. All of our little eras of libbing and rights have a season. Before the dust settles, women, you're up. And, you're not capable of enough bitch for what the male species will dish out to the female onslaught.

Can't we all just get along?

Only if we want to.

We cannot bring this much poison to the playing fields of love and relationships and expect to "get along". It is wrong to talk "get along" with relationship daggers and AK-47s behind our backs. Even a gentleman has a breaking point.

Comprehensively speaking, the sex files have many sides to them. Sex and REALationships is as simple as basic respect for humanity but more complex than the trillions of neurons that play us.

CHAPTER 15
"LET'S OPEN THE DIALOGUE"

We cannot open the dialogue with smoking guns ablaze or a sharp shooter waiting in hiding: waiting for Mr. Sexual Misconduct, Mrs. Student Underage Sex Offender and Mr. Rapist to "come out".

1. They smell our smoking guns like a fox smells a trap.
2. No one's dialoguing with a gun to their head or if they think it's a trap to take them out.

If it's dialogue, it is not a trial. Dialogue is good, but what are we talking for? If it is to collect evidence or print his story of shitty sex practices, we are lying to ourselves and everyone else. People don't step into fake dialogue with bombs like sexual improprieties in their closets. It is unfair and it is wrong to use everything he says or does in our biased courts of law on the media stage to bring the bastards down if it is "dialogue". If it is a lynch mob, we should inform the harassers, so that they do not show.

We've sat on sexual crimes for thousands of years and suddenly have the urge to binge on annihilating the bastards who commit such heinous acts. The systems and societies that have used the sexual pasts of people and paid to keep her quiet suddenly have this great compassion for victims. "What the hell is going?"

Really! What's behind the sudden craving to clean house. When we sit presidents with scandal in the public eye then go for his jugular and ignore others, why are we suddenly on a big red bandwagon of sexual crimes? How does 2018 go down in history with the Most Influential being the face of Sexual Crimes? There is nothing wrong with the Most Influential being the face of Sexual Crimes, but what is wrong with this? Is it really because there is a bigger agenda to take out the current powers-that-be? Why is The Institution (the systems behind the systems) so afraid of the current presidents and leaders? There is something to fear.

Yes, maybe some victims are having a voice, but once again, in many cases, the systems and institutions prey on the victim for its own ends. Are victims just means to an end? That in itself – using victims' stories for agendas – is another victimization of victims. We continue to say how silencing victims is so wrong. Using their stories for our tainted agendas is more wrong. (All agendas are not tainted.) Victims get to say this happened or that: and be validated. When victims are pawns in any game, once again, they are being used. More noble is, "You are valuable because you are" and "Your story is vital for you to heal". Shitty is, tell your story so that we have more ammo to bludgeon Mr. Sexual Crime. Victims get thrown under the bus to use their story to take Mr. Sex Crime Power Player down for the benefit of someone else.

How do we suddenly grow a conscience on sexual crimes and the world be subject to our sudden conscience? Many of the institutions, systems, agendas and power players knew The Bad Sex Story of him and her for years. Many of them made bank or position from his bad sex story or hers. Who makes The Institutions, systems and power players accountable? How do we let sexual crimes play out for years and wake up one day to take out all of "the guilty"? Who made the rules that now is the time? What was the intent? If the intent was to knock off the Good Old

Boys' Club, it is futility - we will have boys clubs.

Why are the guilty players in institutions, power circles, leaders of nations and kingdoms exempt from the rules and laws that apply to Mr. Bastard over there? If you have a rule, enforce it when things go down. The fact that no one did anything and we suddenly have the urge, says our motives for so doing are suspect. There is a severe injustice being perpetrated on victims and perpetrators.

Victims want resolve, reform. When we poison the victims' message of resolution and reform with hate, we add to the irreconcilable mayhem that already exists. It is like killing the addict because he is an addict instead of slaying his demons. Every sex offender or sexual crime individual is not an addict. Most of the agendas are not seeking resolution. They are destroyers. A destroyer will always have a foe, an enemy, a war. Make sure you have the right arsenal on your side when you wage wars. Hate has a way of imploding.

At the point that you are a hater, know which cause you're representing. You've defeated the purpose of your cause if you represent it with such hatred, no one wants to hear you. You're a liability. Every human being has a right to be here; to be heard: if they want to be heard: if anyone is listening. The world that you need to hear stops its ears when you kill them first. The dead cannot hear. Your audience is limited because:

You're biased.

You don't even know all of the story.

You don't even care about all of the story.

You don't tell the whole story – including the story of your perpetrator.

Nobody (perpetrators nor the accused) wants to go down like that.

Nobody wants to be treated unfairly.

The powers-that-be holding all the cards would do anything to save their own asses.

The powers-that-be – whether agenda or persona - cannot be trusted.

There is an entire story. Most of us have only heard one side – the side we want them to hear to kill the bastard. What's the other side of the stories?

CHAPTER 16
BIGOTS OR BULLYING?

Do you remember when you did the most unpardonable, jaw-dropping, parents-blood-veins-showing-in-the-temples, infuriating thing you could possibly do? This one was not even on your parents' radars. They met you at the door trembling (with anger that was boiling the coagulated blood in their capillaries). Your mind was blank from shock and you didn't even know that you had already passed out from fright.   When you revived they were still asking the loaded question.

"What (in God's name) were you thinking!!!!!!?"

OR

"Why? Why? ...?!" OR "How could you do this to me and your mother?"

The screaming "why" turned on the neighborhood lights.

If from somewhere in your brain-paralysis of fear you could even manage to move your lips to answer, their mouth curled even further and they roared from killer anger, "You better SHUT-UP <Jack!>" If you could look, you'd see the silhouette of neighbors at their windows opening them to see what Jack did.

Well, we've done the same thing with our invitation to the Sex War forum. We've invited the whole world to the table with invitations engraved in generations of sex corruption and demanded that they sit down and shut the hell up! We've told them how to respond to us if they dared say anything about the new sex revolution. If anyone were possibly stupid enough to try to say anything about this current crisis, we rolled them over with a 200-ton bulldozer like rolling over a vexatious gnat on summer's eve.

How dare they!!!

It is fair and right that women and men get to tell their story. It is unfair for us to tell the public how to feel, what to say and what to do about his story or hers. We cannot boss the public around. The whole truth will require victims to account for their role (if any) in how their story happened. It will ask parents some pointed questions about the sex pain of their children. Comprehensive approaches dig it all up to heal it. Otherwise our passion, hashtags, organizations and causes are just patches. And bad sex will continue.

Whatever our stories, our sexual justice advocates don't get to police the world and tell everyone else what to do, how to feel, to resign, to step down, to commit suicide (professional or otherwise). Here goes bullying again. Every individual has a right to make decisions about what they will do and how they respond within the parameters of fair (or unfair) and within the parameters of the law. Bullying the public about what they can and cannot do when a story is told steps over the cliff.

That hostility is another strike against the champions of the Sexual Harassment, Sexual Assault and other Sexual Justice movements.

The law decides. The opinionated circus hurts the cause and presents a side of bullying we wouldn't dare call bullying. We don't get to police the world. In so doing, we provoke hatred from even the most neutral of us. As bad as any level of sexual misconduct is, sexual rights bigots and bullies feed hate. It is still hate.

There is no fair playing field to resolve if we are acting like this – bossing the public around. If we hope to resolve the sexual crimes crisis, include instead of isolate. If we make men feel like shit, they're not coming to our table. Yes, of course, they made the women or men feel like shit when they victimized them, but shit is still shit.

It is shitty for perpetrators to live with themselves and in our societies. We hate women bashing. We are now male bashing. And, we are demonizing the people who can possibly assist. Some of us destroy, intentionally.   Sorry to say, but we're not just attacking Mr. Sexual Harass. At this point and with the vehement hatred that we present to the bastards, it's beginning to feel a lot like an attack on being man.   It feels like an attack on having the right to form an opinion of your own. People are leery to trust our stories if they can't hear all of it or if they think that we are being unfair to all of the other parties involved.

Our audiences judge what they do not hear as much as what they hear. The fact that we may not say our whole story leaves big question marks. Why aren't we saying all of our story? Are we hiding something? What are we hiding? As wrong as sex crimes are, if we are to win, we must come big. Be fair, especially to the people who want to help resolve this crisis; especially to those who want to hear.

CHAPTER 17
SAY IT LOUD

Hands down, women should have a voice. But, what are we doing with it? Women have a right to be angry about what happened there. Sometimes we can only say it in anger. The difference between having a voice and seething hate is as vast as our extreme right and left opinions.

Does our intense quest for sexual justice come from a relentless passion for what is right and equitable and good, or a seething hatred of him? If it is a relentless passion for what is right and equitable and good, may we be fair and impartial. May we be right and equitable and good in our cause and our pursuits. If our intense quest for sexual justice comes from hate, where does the hate come from? Is it because of what he did? Is it because we can't get justice? Is it because we really hate ourselves? Or, is our hate rooted elsewhere? Does your burning hatred rot your core more than it brings him to justice? May the hate bring you to healing instead of chronic poison that curses your life.

The hatred we're breathing is an infectious contagion that has become pandemic. The hatred is being reflected back at women and causes whose means and methods deeply perturb the wider population. This reflected hatred from our public isn't necessarily directed to men and perpetrators only. Even where women are victims, the hate perpetrated on the wider community by the sexual justice causes breeds hatred back. Does the wider community hate the women or victims? Not necessarily. Maybe they hate the methods, means and implications.

Unfortunately, the voice of sexual justice is being tainted. Unfortunately, when we taint the voice with hatred, we spread hatred and it is so much harder to listen. Unfortunately, when we taint the voice with hatred, most people cover their ears to protect their heart from the mutilation of hatred. In our racial wars when white bigots punch black or black bigots pummel white, we cringe from something inside that insists, "That ain' right". In our sexual wars where hate is louder than seeking justice, we incite the world to hate back.

And, maybe (for some of us) it isn't the women, the men nor the cause we hate so profoundly. Maybe we hate that thing inside of us that tends toward "kill": we slay one another with that side of us that is counterproductive to who we all are: humanity. Maybe we hate that as civilized people, we still live incapable of solving our differences like civilized people. Maybe we hate that the powers-that-be, with all of their damn power, cannot resolve such issues without this level of chaos. Maybe we hate that, once again, we are subject to so much brutal hatred without enough honesty and full disclosure (on both sides) to really resolve this. Stop wasting people's time if we're not bringing everything to the table. Stop putting the masses through this level of shit, when our motives and hearts are wrong on so many counts. We have the fact that people are being victimized. We know that and we hate that. What we do not have is the whole truth.

Stories are being told and were told in a tone to share their story, to say their heart, to inform. They are effective. When the story is used like a scalpel, no one is coming to the table. When the story has ulterior motives and other agendas, Sexual Justice advocates discredit themselves and victims.

Abusing the victim by misusing their voice, disrespects the victims of sexual crimes. This was not the intent of movements. Unfortunately, movements are being used for this: not just by the movement, but by politicals and critics. When the goal is to solve the problem and not kill the bastards, more people may listen better and support more.

As long as we are on a warpath to drive the male species to extinction, our movement is limited. Hatred breeds hatred. Of course, have a voice if you wish. Even if all you can do is say it in hatred and anger now, we have a right to say it or not. Get a voice and say your story, but what is it for? How is sexual misconduct addressed and solved more productively without killing the bastards who gave you a "dirty look"? If we do not change the course of our movements, our greatest weapon – sexual justice - will destroy us.

"So don't take the bastards down?"
"Where is your heart, sister?"

In other words, if you can take a bastard down and be the full potential of you at the same time, you may have a point. The war is bloody and dirty, though. After taking the bastards down, Woman must still confront woman. There is so much to do inside of us, we can miss a lifetime of greatness on a bastard. Not to mention, the spoils of war that infect the soul of us add to the piles of insecurities, resentment, bitterness, guilt, fear and hatred in Woman.

Can you lift that?
"What?"
The piles of debris from the years of hatred, insecurity and abuse.
"Of course, I can lift it! I'm Woman!"

It's not whether we can lift it or not. We can. One of the most looming questions is, "What is lifting that doing to you?"

Angry Pain

It is critical to reiterate that the discussions about women abusing the movements are for those who do. Can we have platforms that resolve the problems instead of kill the men? Sometimes we can only scream our story because it hurts so much, but it is so much easier to hear a woman who presents her story in a way to be understood: instead of a way to kill.

We hear the stories. We have heard the stories. There are more stories to hear, more stories to tell. Some of us can separate the pain from the anger. Some of us get so offended by the anger, we cannot pay attention to victims' pain. The pain gets silenced to offended ears but the pain still has a voice.   Our story is once again less impactful if the anger is that offensive. The anger is loud: so loud that we cannot hear the pain. The pain is actually more effective when expressed the right way. Sometimes, even if it does not come out the right way, the heart behind it carries it where it needs to be well enough to be effective. Everyone does not need to hear. If the right person hears, that is all that matters.

One of the tolls on the human life from our sex corruption is losing one's soul to the powers-that-be behind the scenes of our inner struggle. There are so many powers-that-be behind the scenes: the hate, the greed, the systems, the people in charge of the systems. We try to answer our questions about why we are, who we are, how we are and what we are without any knowledge of the forces that play behind the scenes. We refute truth because we seldom realize that we are up against other forces in our life equations. The fact that there are other forces and systems at play behind the scenes of sexual victimization does not mean that perpetrators are not responsible for what they did; it does not mean that victims stories are less important. The fact that there are other forces behind the scenes of sexual victimization means that these forces need to be considered and resolved as well. Anything we cannot live without – sex, lies, dope, whatever your vice – is rooted in what is stronger than us. If indeed, we are really after, "What is wrong with me? How do I fix this?", we must consider why we are out of control (if we are).

CHAPTER 18
BITCHES, WITCHES, BASTARDS & WIZARDS

There are no bitches, witches, bastards and sorcerers, really. There's a person under there. The layers we put on to get through life cover up the person inside. To survive, to get, to live, to do, we sometimes get "dirty". Some of us get so dirty, we look like bitches, witches, bastards and wizards. Sexual profession or banker, if we choose to adapt to evil, it can get inside. Even beneath that, there is a person inside.

People get marred by the places they've been. Some get the demons into their soul; some get away; some die there. There is still a human soul in the vilest beast of a She Badass, and Sorcerer King was born a man.

The only way to break the cycle of our years-gone-by, is to stop. Many of us can't just stop. Inside, we are all human. Even a she-devil has humanity under there: a he-devil too. Unfortunately, the deficits pile up. We forge on with the hurt and every single place bleeding inside. Instead of healing, we create a world with the hurt, from the deadly pain and demon-sized anger. These are our foundations. Then we roar at the rest of the "normal" "jackasses" in the "normal" world. And, everyone else (except for us) is a jackass.

Breathing Pain

The pain is deep: so deep. We gasp for air just to breathe to live.
This is how we walk. This is how we survive. This is life. The
pain of bad sex past is as an incurable disease. Sometimes we
whelp. Sometimes we scream. Sometimes we are just panting.
Not from our abating strength but from the breathing pain. The
pain keeps us alive. It is how we feel. It is all we feel. We cannot
feel anything else.

The pain is brutal. We are brutal. Some of us bear it silently.
Some of us scream its brutality all over the world. The world is
offended by our brutality. But the pain is excruciating. It's
excruciating so we come swinging our stench at the world. We're
crying for help, really.

There is no help from mediocre places, O Afflicted.

They cannot help us with pain this ancient, this merciless, this
deadly. They cannot help you. The money can't help us enough to
stop Pain's breath. The money cannot make us whole. And, even
if we say it loud in one voice, the pain is still there in the echoes of,
"Help me!"

We need to be held by love. We don't even know that, because the
pain makes us blind. And, you cannot hold pain. The world
cannot hold pain this size. The pain will brutalize anything that
touches it. There is a queen in there, though. If ever she can
realize that, she will do whatever it takes to come out of Pain's
hell. But the pain is stronger. It's fiercer. It's more powerful than
she.

These BIG filthy places are so deadly, they're treacherous. And
depending on how we go the course, we emerge Queen or Beast.

Beast thunders at the world so menacingly, the world shrouds itself. The world cannot even come to a place to try to understand. The world covers its ears and its heart in self-protective mode. Beast is a level of self-righteousness that has nothing to do with church nor "the righteous". Beast's self-righteous is deadly. Oh self-righteousness is not an insult. It is *our* pain and we get to conduct it how *we* choose. Not only that, YOU (the rest of the world) must listen. The world cannot hear you from where it hides from the stench of Beast's death pain.

Owning the pain: people are holding pain as their own so tightly in their bosom, it's eating their flesh. It's all of our pain, really. We decide if it's worth our life or if we let it go. It is too much. The pain of bad sex past is too much to carry. It will kill you, literally: sometimes eventually.

No, he doesn't get away with it if you let him go. How could it be that he rose to house, senate or the billionaire list after what he did? Every legal system of justice has failed, every attempt, every silence. Our screaming has failed. So we drag him to the office of public opinion and try to slay him there. Like a speedy, slithering roach, he got away again. He never really gets away.

It's not about letting him get away. It's about having something left inside you to find the strength to walk on ... Walk on.

CHAPTER 19
INFLICTOR AND THE WOUNDED

The many-sided conflicts of our sex crimes and stories are (in part) about the Inflictor and the Wounded. If we could see what really haunts us, we would see that there is no way that we can go it alone. We need help. Asking for help takes humility but the pain makes us angry. You need help with that. Even if screaming the pain is a part of healing, it mutilates our flesh so violently, it leaves us for dead. Many of us take on another vengeance. This vengeance doesn't just kill the bastards in our wake. It kills victims too.

Don't let the pain kill you with resentment so poisonous it takes you out. It is necessary to heal. It is life to forgive. Forgive yourself. We even need to forgive him or her: if we want to live the best life. The unforgiveness turns into a bitter toxin that is so poisonous it becomes flesh-eating (qualify: this is not about people with medically diagnosed flesh-eating conditions that come from other).

Don't die there, Sister – in flesh-eating hell. Come away from there. The only way to stop breathing the pain is to come away from it. Deal with it. Be wise but deal with it. Deal with it wisely and come away. Come away and breathe life. You'd better find life or breathing pain will kill you. You're worth more than that.

Queen wins. The pain makes queens or it makes demons. You weren't born to die. The furnace of great pain is a burn that makes pure gold depending on our journey through. The crushing makes fine wine; the press makes oil too valuable for price. You are more than a scar. You are Queen. You were born a she. The pain, the struggles, the woundings are the making of Queen.

Is there some other way?

Perhaps. Perhaps there are other ways for a lesser you. For those of us who don't settle, there was no other way.

> Sex File
> Jacquard
>
> Jacquard told her story today. Her father was murdered when she was 3-years-old and she had no relationship with her mother. Her life spiraled to bitch status living from those places. Jacquard went from international drug trafficking to prison.

Just because you land in prison or sign up for the drug trade does not make you a bitch.

We stand at the crossroads at least once. Sometimes the pain leaves us so toxic, we become venomous poison. At the place where we revel in being She-Badass, we've given ourselves over to kill. Bitches and witches prefer to marry satan and die there happily. Bitches and witches are intentional in killing men. Bastards are intentional in killing women. There are degrees of bitches, witches, bastards and demon-possessed sorcerers. There is a point of no return.

Most of us don't know how to struggle for power without being bitchy for the most part. And maybe, bitchy is required to take over places men and women factions are trying to steal. You steal what you don't own. There is sufficient possession for everyone. It is so inhumane to want his or hers. Get your own power. When you have to take his or hers, you don't know yours; and, some men and women are just evil – they want it all; not because they want it. They cannot imagine that you have something: power, money, status or fame.

"The struggle is real".

What struggle are you struggling? That is not your struggle if you're after her family inheritance or the corporation he built. Go for your own greatness. We end up in struggles that are not ours talking about "the struggle is real" to convince ourselves that what we are doing is so worthy. You're wasting your time. Whatever win you get is temporary. You cannot own what is not yours. Eventually, you lose.

There is nothing more beautiful than a she-devil coming to the end of herself and living her purpose. Jacquard took the long road back. It took many years in prison and coming face-to-face with her choices to find her rock bottom, but she did. There she found her humanity: the layers of Queen inside that got covered up. The world could hear her pain above her anger that looked like bitchiness.

Even a She-Devil can become a queen. Jacquard was "lucky". As Divalicious and bodacious as our she-divas and as popular and famous, it is impossible to find one as sexy as Jacquard.

CHAPTER 20
SALACITY

The extreme and juicy pleasure that we get from his downfall is evil. There is a satanic happy that some of us get when one of the big bitch-bastards fall. We love it like popcorn and an epic blockbuster. That is how we enjoy the show of Mr. Power Player bites the filthy dust of filthy sex shame.

Oh! 'Tis wonderful! Wonderful! Wonderful!

We rub our hands together, pull up our favorite, worn chair with the ottoman and stretch out in deep comfort to watch the bitch-bastard drop. With glee, we suck up the sensation of his demise like a turn-on, eat it up, drink a toast with his haters and grin that we were RIGHT! Yes! He *did* do it! Yes, I told you so! Yes! Yes! Yes! Yes! A pump of victory for us and a pile of any other lingering television headlines that social media has not buzzed about him. If he squirms, that is all the better. We squeal! It's a delight squeal. The bitch-bastard went down!

There is a major difference between seeking justice and being malicious. The institution uses the sex card to control its power players. It's the institution that sends the prostitute your way sometimes, Power-Player. Our current sex-gaming things discredit the stories that are true and plays a game in which nobody wins. What is worse is the institution's double standard. Taking no-tolerance stances on sexual improprieties and covering up all of the other dirty secrets is a double standard. Taking one bastard down and leaving the others standing is a double standard. Why should Joe Blo be required to obey the law?

Sexual impropriety versus other criminal activity is not about comparing sexual improprieties to other issues in any way. There are no comparisons, except for the common thread – they are all wrong. So spit out all of the wrong while we're sex shaming. Let's have a healthy dose of grand theft shaming scandals, cheating out that opponent at whatever duel headlines, or viral clips about how our choice party drugs cost 3-year-old Carlos IV his father's life by the cartel.

Who makes the rules? Why should a public trust an establishment who covers up anything? When people lose faith in the establishments that waste their power, people tend to support something or someone else.

For years establishments have used sex to manipulate the power game and the power struggles. Oh, who will admit to this? To do so robs the power players holding the sex card of their power. If this is not the case, push all of the rest of your shit to the media and the headlines. Yes, tell the world about the big bad money games and market plays behind the scenes; not let them find out. Tell them about international weather warfare, germ and climate warfare that the big boys play at the expense of human lives. Climate control? Talk about the missiles in the sea that possibly quake the earth and can release energy systems powerful enough to affect climate change. Keep on recycling your bottles and go green, but we'd better start looking at all of the games on this planet. What else do we blame on humanity when other powers are at work? What else do we blame on him or her, when there are other factors to consider: some with more dire consequences. Play these cards the same way we play the sex card. Push all of the dirt out. Who's standing?

Salacity is spicy scandalous fare.

CHAPTER 21
EMPOWERMENT

Women! Women! Women! Produce your empowerment! You are gifted and endowed with mega skills, potential and ability! Stop settling!

Sex File

She accuses him of rape and of sexually assaulting her 4 times. She has had consensual sex with the accused. The accused denies her allegations and claims that she is accusing him to extort money from him.

Once again, Ladies: If we want to solve our current sex crisis, we have to bring it: all of it.

Please get this: There are too many unanswered questions, too many missing details and too many people shouting at the rest of the world to sit down, shut up and take what they say at face value.

How do you get alone in the space of someone who sexually assaulted you a second time? (Caveat: Many children and teens live daily in sexual abuse environments that are their homes. We are not talking about children, nor teenagers). The first sexual assault may have been a mistake. But if someone sexually assaults you, why do you attend his space again for any reason? Work, party, confrontation, or group thing. Why? This places our stories in a very compromising juxtaposition to truth. And, the world has to find a place on our side or for us to resolve this sex crisis from events like these.

A third time? A fourth?

If someone hurts you badly enough to call it sexual assault, why do you attend his space again? This is one of the stalemates of our sexual harassment and sexual assault causes. We are not making sense to the world. We know how we date, hang out and be with our crowd/posse or social circles. Even we have protocols of hang out and dating (spoken or unspoken). It looks like you had something and something went wrong; you didn't get what you want out of the relationship. Now you're coming back to take him out. It looks like revenge or a relationship gone wrong. This is not the only case like this. There are too many cases like this. And, one of the worst things about it is, we don't get to say to our sister, "Don't go back there. Stay the hell away from him." That is judging or wrong to say. If you're about to step in a pile of shit, why can't she say, "Whoa! Shit over there!"? Why are women attacking the people trying to assist?

Come on, Women. If we really want to resolve this, we have to look at this with all eyes on deck. We are not trying to resolve the sex crisis. That is evident. If we are trying to resolve this, we have to be straight up honest with ourselves, tell ourselves the truth (not our truth) and work from the truth. You only go back to a relationship space if you like being there or like him. If he hurts you that badly, what do you go back for? Please, please, please don't say, "It was my job." No, no, no. Your job is never to be a sex thing for your employer or anyone. That is not a job. (Unless your job is a sex profession.) If your job is not a sex career, why are sex things happening? If the relationship is more than work, work it out. Even if it is more than work, he should not be sexually assaulting you.

Many of the sexual misconduct, etcetera, happened for years in the same environment. Yes, we have to take care of our children. Yes, there are bills to pay. Yes, we want a better life. Yes, we want to live our dreams and accomplish our goals. But you cannot afford to lose yourself in the process! Keep your dignity.

Life opens doors for you when you know who you are. When you stay in places of sexual crimes, you say it is okay that this is happening. You accept sexual crimes. Oh we like to keep going and we like to get a step up. Make your own ladders! Not even the powers-that-be in charge of the sex game are finding a place for you on their bottom rung. If it's your ladder, you own it. You climb if you want to or sit on the third rung if you're happy there. If it is yours, they have to climb: not you.

It is amazing that many of us who accept an offer – a job, a gift, money – from a dirty Harry, always go back for more. There may be times when it is necessary to get things done (legally) from dirty Harry, but when this is a preference, check your heart codes. Why do you prefer to aggravate dirty Harry than make your own life happen? There are ways to find your own way. If you have to pump dirty Harry for a better job or a necklace, he's ahead in his game. Get your own things in kosher ways. It may be a lesser job but nobody owns you.

The player who uses you strengthens his foul sex game and taking from him with your ulterior motives is more harmful to you. Not to mention, you develop a mentality to *get* like that. Just because she made it playing like that, doesn't mean that you will. Many takers who try to work dirty Harry still don't have: some still play the game. They do not own themselves. Someone will always own you. No matter how much bank you embezzle out of the last man, you do not own yourself. At the very least, the money owns you. A slave to the money is still a slave. At the end of the day, you're not free.

The powers inherit or get their power somehow. Whatever privilege, hard work or swindle your forefathers did to get you where you are, use it to facilitate people empowering themselves or get the hell out of the way. It is one thing not to help someone get theirs. It is another to literally oppose them. Hello satan. You answer to a higher power. Everyone does.

May your power player that you must answer to be on your side. There are power players who disdain the "weak" – Hitler trait. There are power players who help the "weak" for their own gain – Opportunists and Users. There are real philanthropists in this world. They help the less fortunate because they genuinely want to. If you're taking advantage of women's positions to screw them, you are playing games with the devil. The devil has this tendency – he must win at any cost.

CHAPTER 22
WHO ARE YOU SEXING?

"Trust me!" He says.
"You don't trust me!" She says back to him.

"Do you trust me?" [He asks his beau that.]
"Of course, I trust you." [His beau lies through his teeth.]

We continue to demand and try to pull trust from places and people devoid of it. We don't even trust ourselves. You cannot trust what you do not know. We cannot expect another to trust what they do not know. Fast forwarding backwards to the beginning, we *became* naked and ashamed. Before that, we were buck naked and didn't even know that we were naked.

Shame comes from knowledge of ... In this sex case, it is knowledge of guilt. What did you do? What did we do? Shame says, there is everything wrong with you. Shame says, "You did that". So we live shame. The world keeps shaming people. It is so much more dramatic to be Shame and to make the bastards pay. They say, "You owe your life, Dude!" One of the worse things about Dude is, he is buying into their sentencing of him and trying to pay. No matter how much you charge him for what you say he did, he cannot pay for that.

Perverse

He cannot be intimate with you because he is ashamed that you
will see him and do a Connive – exploit his vulnerability to get an
advantage over him: learn his secrets so that you can control him
(to do what the dark side does). Intimacy requires seeing the
hidden secrets of. The dark side cannot see the truth about him and
cover it; that is a love way – to cover his bad truth. The shame
way operates as it is. Shame just is, as love just is. While love is
covering the results of our indiscretions, shame is exploiting it.
This is one of the biggest problems with the current sex crisis –
people exploiting other people's shame for their gain.

Don't expect for shame to cover your unglorious. That is why she
does not trust you. Fundamentally, he cannot trust you, because
you operate from shame. Shame takes daggers to the weak and the
strong; love heals.

Sides

Shame lives on the bad sex side of things. Love keeps us on the
sexy sex side of things.

Who you sexing?

Don't be sexing someone on the shame side of things and expect
for them to play you like love. He is going to play you like Shame:
you lost your freedom or gave it away. We lose our freedom when
we become the slave to something or someone else. So we see
ourselves as what we did, act like what we did and sex people from
what we did – shame.

Why are you carrying him?

For thousands of years women have carried the stigma of being
worthless. As priceless as it is to carry, bear, born and nurture a
child, women have been beaten down and re-reminded that they

are worthless. As priceless as it is to be queen, women have been treated as worthless. As priceless as it is to invent, pioneer and master our professions, women have been treated as worthless. So we've carried the shame. Women have taken revenge by manipulating the bastards; women have used our child-bearing card to control the bastard hungry for children; some of us have flung our sexy femininity back to the God who gave it. We hang out in the space of "I'm Woman" with no foundation for our "I'm Woman" worlds and lose what is our ruff card – femininity.

Oh no! Femininity is not weak, nor placid. It is Queen. Our greatest fight is that – to be Queen. It is an unnecessary fight because you don't have to fight to be who you are. We're fighting for the wrong things. Designer purse and bag: red sole shoes and purchased gun-cased hips: fame and famous men by our side: does not make queen. You are queen.

We have our own domain, influence and scepter in this world. Is there a war that needs to be waged against the bastards? Be careful not to give the bastards all of your power fighting them. We can win better by reveling in the fact that we are Queen. Get your own empires and own your own conglomerates. Taking his little company is so mediocre compared to what you have; and it is such negative energy, it stifles your power to be who you are – Queen.

We carry him and "what he did to me" in our energy, in our persona, in our bodies. He's too heavy. How do we free up? First, love yourself. Love yourself enough to set yourself free. The hate keeps him tied to your back. You can make more progress without the load on your back. Does he just get away with it? No. Here comes trust. The dirty T word says trust that he will not get away with it.

So, here we are policing the world and nations with our Bastard Hate agendas so deep and rampant, we can't even discover our

Queen inside. The hate is venomous poison boiling the temperature of women to a blazing fever that is so destructive to women, we are ineffective in the Bastard War. Yeah, women may take a few of the bastards down but if he turns us into a witch during the process, you're that much further from Queen.

Today there are unicorn power-player companies pioneered and owned by women. Go for yourself Queen! Instead of bitching, find a way to go for yourself.

CHAPTER 23
GENDER EQUALITY

Sex File

He caught his "girl" with his "friend". His rage incited him to bang on the windows to get inside until he broke the glass. Before he could assault his friend and/or his "girl", they escaped. He pursued before he returned to remove his belongings from the house where he lived with his "girl".

It's over but he wants his "girl" back. He cheats on her with multiple sex partners but wants her back.

This sounds like one of those extreme TV shows. It may be too melodramatic to fit all of our shitty "relationship" profiles, but the fundamentals are the same. Sometimes we need to see the extreme to see that what we have is either headed in the same direction or has all of the basic characteristics to become the same. We need to understand that anything less than the best is unacceptable or to see that our thing with him is shit on a more subtle level. We need to see that any of our compromises tell him, he can get away with more. We consciously or subconsciously say, man and woman are not equal and that it is fair or all right for women to be treated lesser.

His "girl" is his possession like one of his game box joysticks that he tosses somewhere under the unkempt sofa with the bag of chips, the unfinished pizza, the roaches and the occasional sewer rat. There is really no relationship here. There is nothing vested, nothing to fight for, except for his slave "girl" to keep. His slave "girl" is there: for his rage and emotional baggage, to cook him what he likes if she feels like it and to make sure he has clean jocks to wear to sex his other "girls" across town. Occasionally, he pumps her busted vagina with his STDs that he picked up from his "girls" across town and beats her to get a makeup sex rise.

You earn respect. Respect is not taken. Even if you take your respect from him or her, it's not respect you take. You respect yourself; you get respect from those who are honorable enough to give respect. Respect is mutual. With a gun to his head, he may FEAR you *temporarily*, but you've made yourself more into a "crazy bitch" than someone who's earned his respect. FEAR is not respect.

When women, without permission, create nations, economies, 10G networks, gamechanger companies, we don't NEED to demand respect. They *see* that we just are – leaders, authority, royalty, fierce. Respect just happens. Why do you NEED respect so? You would hunt a bastard down and try to exact it from him. Dig in. Dig into your own soul and find out what you missed that makes you so ravenous for respect, you'd try to take something that cannot be taken. Then respect yourself enough to heal thyself and your life, and go for Queen.

Some of our greatest female artist idols sing about their man tactics and getting a man. Some of our greatest male artist idols sing about how many women they hump a night, play at the same time, or how many "pussies" they have. Our daughters sing the song of the female idols; some of them sing the song of the male idols too.

FEMALE IDOL SONG: Come get my juice, Baby.

MALE IDOL SONG: I done played that. I pump you, ya bestie, ya mama and the menage a mille all night.

Our sons sing the song of the male idols and the female ones. The song gets in their heart. Our heroes sing songs that program the heart to be disrespected and to disrespect. We've learned to think that way. It's inevitable. We don't have to believe; it's all around us.

We've fought for gender in-equality from there were men and women on the planet. Today is now. It's time to change the fight. You cannot talk gender equality and disrespect yourself. He will never treat you as his equal if all you are is a pussy to him.

A queen does not fight for what she owns. She owns it. Your first possession is yourself. If we cannot possess that, we are ill-equipped to own what is rightfully ours. If we cannot own our bodies, he will. She cannot barter with her body and it remain hers. Her body is in the system. There is something more to that. We're so blindsided and busy fighting for our souls back from the systems of "men", we are lost in a chaotic tailspin of power playing that we are still losing. Get it – we cannot give it up to him without losing some piece of us that we will spend ourselves trying to redeem: until we come to some level of peace with our-SELF. Your body is tied to your soul – your self-esteem, your self-respect, your emotions and your will. Even the She Badass comes to this realization at some point.

Your other possessions are the gifts and abilities that are uniquely yours and only yours. You have inside you gifts and abilities priceless enough to stand before kings (because of your non-sex related gifts and abilities). Fight with everything you have to develop them!

Not every woman is suffering from gender inequality. Again there are enough of us in high places to make our own difference instead of men bashing.

Watch your "queens". Look at the women who own their domain. Men come to them to be a part of their businesses and economy. They're not fighting with men kingdoms, nor groveling to get a nut. They get their own nuts! Get your own nuts! (Not balls.) The balls just come when you have your own nuts. It takes a secure man to be with a queen, but if women are that secure, we will up the ante on how much more secure our men have to be.

Men, why do women have to haunt you to get gender equality? Why they got to bitch you to get equality? Be the man.

Women have been treated unequally for so long, injustices have taken many women to "take no prisoner" wars. We've awakened the "kill" fight and the collective woman is at kill mode on the sex crimes warpath. Why do women have to bitch men to get equality? Why do we have to awaken a bitch level so inhumane it's annihilating us, in order for women to try to get respect? Be the man.

Is the inequality gap more gaping because we've created an era of men who hate back? After the Gender War will we look around at the casualties with regret or victory? Real victory.

CHAPTER 24
A FAIR PLAYING FIELD

Technically, there are people and entities who are still trying to come out of the eras (mentally) where the workplace was predominantly male.   The fact that we are still fighting for equal pay for men and women is evidence of that.   There are companies that respect women enough to pay them equally to men, or better. The slow equal pay change is centuries old and dinosaurs will come back before we have equality if we continue to breed that belief system – men are worth more than women. It's a belief.

The systems literally just believe that a man should get more. Gender nepotism is as prevalent as the stale air in corporate skyscrapers. It is evident that we root for our own kind. Rooting for our own kind intimates that eventually men will stick together on the current sex crisis. Eventually, brothers fist pump brothers. Women, they may disband for our current onslaught of sexual harassment and sexual injustices, but heart? Heart doesn't just die.

It is noble to fight for rights, women. It is most noble to find your own power. We don't always find our own power fast enough to forego the corporate environments and go straight for doing our own thing our way. It would be nice if the world were perfect.

The fight started from the beginning of us. We've come a long way and made some progress. If we step away from the heat of the struggles, the battles and the wars for equality, we could possibly see the bigger picture. The fact that the prevailing theme – gender inequality - has existed almost forever, means "It ain't about you, Honey!" Like ghosts, something else is in the air. Look behind the scenes.

In part, it is about the same prevailing theme that makes shitty personal relationships – we did it our way: SELFish. He's got his way. She's got hers. Even where the law defines a certain way that is supposed to be fair and impartial, how we get to the finish line is one big party of such individualism, everybody loses. Whatever we won is peanuts compared to where we could be had we journeyed together.

There are the coolest managers in corporate. There are dawgs in corporate who play corporate politics like a presidential race.

Nevermind, Candidate Red or Blue came out on top. The people got lost in the casualties of war a long time ago. Victims are still covered in bloody stories and shame. That side doesn't trust the other side enough to put all their cards on the table. Some women are gaming and some men are gaming on the sex scandal table. Like love, if we cannot come to the table with truth, nobody wins. Why are we playing games? If you are free and clear of underhanded motives, why are you playing?

CHAPTER 25
INTOLERANCE VS DISAPPROVAL

Our "normal" says, "Her mini is just below her ass, so that makes her a "hoe"." A mini just below her ass may be a maxi length dress because her culture is to go naked or to cover genitalia to protect (not hide).

Ignorance sometimes breeds intolerance. "Intolerance" is not always intolerance. Sometimes what appears to be intolerance is just someone disagreeing with whatever choice. It may be that the "intolerant" knows your choice will destroy you and will most likely bleed into society at large: and have a detrimental social impact. This response to our choices is not based in fear but wisdom – that's not intolerance. Intolerance based in fear is different from disapproval that comes from wisdom. If we hate wisdom, there is a price for that too.

Your at-the-knee pencil skirt may be just as foreign to her as her ass-length. In the heart of mutual understanding and humanity, understanding where another's ways and whys come from, makes us more civilized.

It is fascinating that one of the most intelligent cultures in the world has a divide-and-conquer mentality for what they deem sexually abnormal. So, Mr. Power Player who did something fifty years ago, probably in environments that tolerated his "shit" 50 years ago, gets slayed with a show-no-mercy attitude. It is not so much that he did what he did (as criminal or wrong as it may be). It is the intent of the forces behind the scenes. Each sexual crime case is different and should be considered that way. The heart carries the intent of judge-and-jury.

It is at least fascinating that men are being told to control their testosterone-filled dicks while women seduce them in filthy little rags that show their bodies.

To: Ms. Conniving

> Yes, the bodies we bought, worked out for, were born with or stole, is ours.

> Work it, Honey, if that is what you want to do. But when did we get the right to make a man sit his ass down and shut the hell up while we flaunt our pussies in his face?

Apparently, there's nothing wrong with flaunting pussies in his face because we have the right to do with our bodies what we want. Ladies, when we have the audacity to tell them not to address our conniving and slap them with a lawsuit if they even think about disagreeing, we've become what we hate. Bullies or bigots? Bully may sum it up more accurately with our stance to intimidate and coerce because we believe that time's up. i.e. It's time for men to sit the hell down, take the pussy in their face and shut the hell up.

And, men? Maybe you gave up your rights to the She Divas when you gave it up. You always have a right to speak up for or protect yourself. Why are men accepting the male bashing? Just because you looked at her girlfriend with a little side-eye does not give her the right to take your balls. Her girlfriend attending your nightcap was a setup. Wake the hell up, Man! Ms. Conniving loves it that you feel bad so that you can pay her. Find someone good who is worthy of you (your king self). Declassify yourself from the rest of the players and be the man. If men would be the man, women cannot take you down.

Man: Wearing that makes me sexually aroused.

Woman: Control yourself jackass!

Woman, he has a right to say just like you have a right to say.

Control

Ladies, it's one thing to be a women's libber (if you are). It is one thing to get your rights: that is human. It is also another to set a standard for our daughters and our sons. These are all good things. The problem is, it has never stopped there for many of us.

Please excuse yourself from the following if it does not apply.

If you are bringing him down to take control of the proverbial "House" and "Senate", you are in it for the control. You will not win. Again, you are playing a game that is owned by other forces and the nature of their play is to destroy you. They do not lose. Read history. Control will always control you.

Annihilation

If you are going for the "kill", be prepared for the consequences. Again, Annihilator forces are otherworldly like bad karma: like what goes around comes around: like reap what you sow, like... (whatever you learned). Read history. It is one thing to get justice and be fair. It is another thing to sit like the devil enjoying Mr. Power Player's takedown. If that's your thing, you are on the Annihilator's hitlist. Live watching your back. A threat? No. That is just the way it is.

CHAPTER 26
THE SEX TRIBUNAL

Everyone is not a sex racketeering pimp running a sex mafia game. Many men genuinely have a problem. They have a problem with sex, sex etiquette, sex protocols and The Rules. In a society where we look the other way for the sex deviances of the select, we have no right to play sex games with others. What is worse, we are massacring the power player with a sexual "misconduct" problem the same way we massacre the leader of the Sex Mafia. So Mr. He-Looked-at-Her-Ass in the skin-tight pencil skirt mini is being slaughtered the same way as Mr. Sex Mafia. Nevermind, Mr. "He-Looked-at-Her-Ass" wasn't really looking at her; it was a blank stare that happened to be in the same direction as her pose at the coffee station.

We don't sentence robbers the same as murderers in our societies, why are we killing everyone without recourse in our biased sex tribunals? Many of our sex tribunals are a jury of one, the judges are public opinion and the verdict is fixed: GUILTY. There is no trial and no "innocent until proven guilty". Sometimes judge and jury is an institution, a hashtag, a movement. This sudden awakening sounds more like lawlessness but we claim to be a civilized society. ... Not on this one.

We try to rehabilitate criminals, where is rehabilitation needed for sex offenders and where is a life sentence appropriate? Is it really his sex offenses that he is being killed for or the fact that he puts power players' dirty games on the big screen as "entertainment"? It seems our legal system may have inadequacies regarding penalties for sex cases, especially since a lot of Woman Power is deciding the fate of power players.

It is flabbergasting that in a civilized society we haven't enforced laws and order to separate the "bad" men from the good adequately enough to contain the power of undercover targeting select individuals. A man who may have looked at a woman, the chivalry one who mistakenly held the door for her and a brutally merciless rapist, claw around in the same swamp trying to get out. And as much as the law may exist and may have been applied in some silent places, the force of a movement, an organization or cause has allowed such careless slander, the innocent go down with the guilty. The momentum of what may have intended justice has become a malicious weapon for many women and men with sadistically ill-intent. We don't get to just apologize for the cases that go awry. It's like taking a dagger to the heart of an alleged foe and then saying, "Oops, I'm sorry!" He's dead. He cannot even hear you. (Is there forgiveness for these ills? It depends on where we go for forgiveness.) Can forgiveness raise the dead? Maybe, if you're Jesus or so endowed.

There are men who are struggling to recover their life because of a false accusation, or a "dirty" look, or an innocent nod (not because they're into her but because they were trained to be polite to anyone). There are men who have to recover 5,10, 20 years of their lives (or a lifetime) because they are wrongly accused. They were sentenced by the abusers of the momentum of a movement that may have been intended for justice, a hashtag that is a double-edged sword, killer games in the ranks of power players, and/or,

etcetera. There are men who are sorry for the collective "Man";
not because they did something wrong, but because the current
social climate carries a certain stigma that mis-classifies Man. It
mis-classifies the innocent man too because the prevailing hatred
for the sexual demonized men among their species is venomous
toxic gas. Gas is uncontainable without certain bounds; some leak
out. This one has gone global.

It is deplorable that free speech kills. It is despicable that our
freedom binds and bludgeons an innocent person.   It is uncanny
that in a society of civilized people, there is no governance nor
order that directs the momentum of a movement that defies due
process and slays a man: and sometimes, an innocent man.

"Oh, it's just a few. Compared to the amount of sexually assaulted
women, there's no comparison."

Ask the one innocent man who had to pack his one box and leave
his career, company or family. Ask the one whose career is a
public image and it is scattered in shattered pieces around him.
They might say, "One is me. That is too many."

Women, it is not sufficient to say what he did. It is vital to read
your heart places and recognize your intent for attending his space.
However underlying, however unknown, know why you are in his
space like that. And since we are a species who cannot stand to
face ourselves and, like Eve, toss the blame around, it is doubtful
that we will ever look at our own truth about why we are attending
his space like that. Like that: with ill-intent: no matter how
miniscule. If you are attending his space from a pure place, attend.

Woman Power is not necessarily right. Woman Power is
sometimes a front for other powers-that-be and agendas. Woman
Power has shown itself to be political. Political or Joe Blo, many
men really have a sex problem.

The amalgam of America brings men from every background, culture and nation to a world that is different from... We don't just come from somewhere. We embody the culture, the generations, the soul of our origin. People, you don't just change that. Most of us can gel with wherever we go. Where we come from is still in us, though. That does not just go away that easily. And sometimes, it rears its ugly (or pretty) head.

Here is a news flash for us. As long as we are not free, we will have a vice or live numb. And, even Numb relies on anesthetics to keep it alive as the walking dead. Live! is so much more like it! Vibrant! Life-giving! Alive!

Deep down in your soul, you Sexy Man, there is a part of you, if you tap (discover), you will be what you long for – power. The power trips that you take, they're not power; because eventually, they bankrupt you (in some way). Power-tripping is only a cover-up. That is why you still need. It is humiliating to say, "I need", so we humble whomever we take from. The greatest power, king, queen, authority or throne that takes from, takes from others because asking places them at the mercy of. Power and power-trippers don't stoop to the mercy of.

There is a power in humility, though. Truth. Who wants truth? Again, if we remember that with truth comes our greatest power, we may reconsider. There is no tribunal for the man who owns himself. There is more power in a damn sexy thing that you own with your honey than the demise of working a booty call speed dial. There is more power in owning yourself, Man.

CHAPTER 27
THE PROBLEM WITH BEAUTY

We are attracted to beauty by instinct. Our naughty nature moves us to reach out and touch it. Sex is beautiful; he is beautiful; so is she.

What is Wrong with Appreciating Beauty?

There is nothing wrong with appreciating beauty, but there is something wrong with the way we appreciate beauty sometimes; it also depends on the culture and the environment. Where are the lines? Some of the lines are blurred. Some of the rules are vague. And sometimes, save your appreciation for someone who will respect it and not be offended by it. At work, keep walking.

All of us have not been trained to have the right response to what is attractive. And in certain cultures, seeing beauty and saying "You are hot" is a compliment. It does not fly in every culture and with everyone. We beg pardon for those who don't understand the cultures where certain "compliments" are offensive (even a sex crime). May the cultures who've learned it is okay to say, "You're hot!" have a chance to retrain themselves to walk on or respond appropriately?

Foundationally folks? We have a problem. Beauty was created to be appreciated and enjoyed. It was created for so many other things too. Of course, there are people who abuse the privilege to appreciate beauty and nurture it, but we have recreated norms that go against innate propensities – to appreciate beauty, to nurture beauty. It is awkward (at least) when we adapt ways that go against our innate tendencies.

The pressure that we place on our freedom to appreciate beauty (respectfully) changes our fundamentals to other norms that are abnormal to what is instinctively human. It is just human to appreciate beauty. We are bigger than that. We can learn to appreciate beauty respectfully and nurture it.

We go to great lengths to teach and train about saving our mother earth (go for it) and slaughter Mr. Sexual Misconduct instead of training him how to respond appropriately to what he finds beautiful or attractive. How are we training boys to treat girls and girls to treat boys? Why are college-aged freshmen still bobbling over an attractive female? Why does she have to be about sex? How are we training them? Trace Mr. Sexual Misconduct and you will find how he was trained. Trace Ms. Teaser and you will find how she was trained.

Oh, stop with the "innocent", flirty flipping the hair and jiggling the cleavage, ladies (if that is what you are doing intentionally). Many of us have been trained covertly or deliberately to use every God-given and man-given asset we have. Flaunt your assets if that's your thing but be honest about your flaunting enticement. Some men can consider that innocent, but again, some have a jiggling-cleavage-in-my-face issue.

"It's my cleavage!" you say.

They are his eyes.

What if men start saying:

"She was checking out my ass."

"She asked me out and I'm so not interested."

"She gave me the side eye and an unsolicited blink."

What if men take up sexual rights arms in society? Why not?

CHAPTER 28
BAIT AND SWITCH

CAVEATS:

1. Women, whether specifically for seduction to kill or for fashion, you most certainly are allowed to wear whatever you want, wherever you want, whenever you want, however you want. Go naked if you wish.
2. This chapter is not for everyone. It doesn't apply to everyone who paints on their jeans and shows some breasts and thighs.

This is just an FYI, even if you don't give a rat's hairball: There are men who have a really sick sex problem.

One of the ironies of American and other sex cultures is bait-and-switch. We show our lusty breasts and thighs and command men to hold their damn balls. When they come and get it, they get it.

We say, "I'm a woman!"

We say, "I can wear jeans I painted on with my plunging neckline tank that shows my breasts and nips, but don't you even think to look in the general vicinity of my breasts and nips!"

The tight-ass pencil skirt is in at the office. Nevermind, she has to bend over in the tight-ass pencil skirt in his face to pick up a pencil she (mistakenly) dropped. Whether she dropped it by mistake or intentionally, "You'd better keep your hands to your damn self, Man!"

Of course, his sick sex problem is not your problem. Comprehensively speaking though, ...

In light of, many men have a problem with the sex issue, it is necessary to address our "rights" to wear, to be and to do. If you slap him with sexual misconduct when your intent was to seduce him in your tight-ass pencil skirt, what does that make you? A threat? If you did not seduce him (you're just wearing tight-ass... skirt or jeans) and he has a sex-issue like an addict, watch yourself and don't get surprised if he looks at you. Many men's eyes have been trained to look. (Not excusing them: explaining.) Many women have been trained to be look-worthy and more deliberately, to seduce. Many of us get a high out of a look; many think we're "fine". It feels good that someone thinks we look good. Subconsciously, we will tend towards such attention. Unfortunately, it is difficult or impossible to judge the subconscious. If it feels good that he thinks you look "fine", watch out for manipulating his appreciating to your advantage and his downfall.

Some women lie. Simply put, we lie. We can know all we want that we want that attention (subconsciously) and say we don't.

Wear a pilgrim dress then.

"Hell no!"

Pilgrim dress attention is not the attention we want.

Does he not have a free right to say and to be and to do?

What is a double standard and what is not?

"A sexual look is not the same as wearing a tight-ass pencil skirt."

Put the Chocolate Chocolate Chip Cookie in front of the two year old and tell him, "Don't you dare touch that cookie!"

"It's not a child and a cookie we're talking about."

Get this. Please. Get this. Some men are dealing with sex issues so deep, it's like that – a child and a Chocolate Chocolate Chip Cookie.

"Well, he should get help!"

Maybe, so should we. Maybe, Ms. Tight-Ass-Pencil-Skirt needing the attention should address her insecure places. Maybe she should ask herself, "Why do I need him to notice me that bad?"

Where's your Daddy? Where was your Daddy? Every woman doesn't have a missing Daddy problem. Every woman does not have this insecurity. This is to those of us who might. When you needed Daddy attention to nurture your 2-year-old needs, where was he? Speaking of child and cookie, perhaps our need for his attention is childhood attention deficit. At 5, was your Daddy there? What happened that you need Bob at the office to notice you? What are your insecurities?

For whatever reason, Mr. Looky cannot help himself. Our cultures and societies and upbringing have raised systems of men and women who are sexually deranged (according to the standard) and we are most unforgiving of their behavior (rightly so in some instances), but it is vital that we look at the landscape of sex and sexuality comprehensively.

If you don't see that our innuendoes are problems for some men and women, you still do not understand that the sex issue is that deep for him or her.

Of course it's your body and your clothes, but he has a promiscuity problem. His promiscuity definitely is not your problem, but he has one. It is necessary to consider the rules in our societies. Putting a lollipop in front of a 2-year-old and telling them, "Don't touch", is futility.

Our approach isn't from the perspective of we have severe promiscuity and sexually predisposed individuals in our culture. Some of us are deliberately flaunting our asses in their faces with a lawsuit in our greedy little hands. If we really want to fix the problem, we must consider the position that many men have a severe sex problem. If we are really looking for solutions, we would try to figure it out and help them. If it is about the money, we will continue to flaunt our asses in their faces, sue them and watch 'em burn.

What is the HEART behind your tight-ass pencil skirt? No! What is the real heart behind your tight-ass pencil skirt? Go deep and know what is the heart behind your pencil skirt, your painted-on jeans, your cleavage. If your heart is pure, you go for yourself with your tight-ass pencil skirt, painted on jeans and cleavage. But, if there is one tinge of something in you that enjoys (just a little bit) the attention you get from it, trace that. Trace that and BE FAIR!

No one is allowed to impinge upon our free rights to wear and to say and to be and to do.

In the words of Anonymous "My Brother, if you have a sex problem, when you go to work sit dewn, shut the hell up and do your damn work. Oh! And then go the hell home! Straight home, Man!"

Even if you don't have a sex problem or promiscuity problem:

watch yourself.

CHAPTER 29
LIABILITIES AND ASSETS

Feminism is a wonderful thing. It is a necessary thing. Economic, social and political equality of the sexes is a very broad feminism definition. And it is unfortunate that we have to fight for rights. The movements and organizing for feminism are steps in a good direction. How we move and organize for feminism could place us years in the wrong direction. Using causes to grow their corrupt power is an archaic strategy of the institutions and powers-that-be. Societies and institutions (especially of men) are well-versed in using the enemy to accomplish their goals. Welcome to The Sex War.

Woman you are Queen.   There are women who use feminism to justify their KTB (Kill the Bastard) causes. Being woman is honorable and sexy. Be woman. If your woman is abusive to men, that is not feminism. Make sure your feminism is not a coverup for hating men, getting his job, his company or his position. There are enough high places to sit, companies to create and positions to lead. Get your own shit. True woman is queen enough to be secure enough to respect Man and whatever his strengths because she owns her game: even if Man is an Alpha Man. True woman is queen enough to get her own game. Get game. Stealing, killing, lying and cheating to get his is as criminal as the last felonious; that's not feminism neither.

Yes women! We have everyone's attention. Use your power wisely. The rate of this fight is on track for retaliation. What is the point of making progress and taking another era back because we trip over our quests for progress (some, for power)? Fair is fair and wrong is wrong. If you fight dirty, you get dirty results. When we lose our humanity in any event, we destroy the power of our own gamechanger. The gamechanger becomes a bitch.

Instead of sitting around conniving and trying to take their things, help a sister out if you got game, Queen Sister. There are sufficient women with game to make a difference helping women. Part of the curse is, instead of us using our money, resources, time and personas to help other women, we are using it to slay men. That is what makes this a bitch. You have. You know. YOU do! You have, you know, you do if you wish, but use it to contribute to what is equitable; or keep your power.

The fact that women have and know (the sexual harassment story) and are attacking men says this a'in' about the cause (in many cases). Many times, this is about destruction because we have the power to do what facilitates solutions that are fair to everyone. If you sow destruction, you will reap destruction. If this is really about the cause, focus your fight, your passion, your resources, your will on women and helping women.

So, men don't have to pay? Where does it say, sexual misconduct gets the death penalty? What is fair? The spirit, the motive, the "karma", is kill, not fix. Hey Kill Bill, two can play that nasty game! There are sufficient men who want to fix the problem. Work with them on it, instead of annihilating their species. Sooner or later, the good guys feel slighted for their gender. This will only backfire.

What if men said, "Shit. We've had enough of this shit! We're not taking it anymore!"

What if they say, "I worked my ass off for this company to provide opportunities, to support and assist economy, women and my nation"?

> Sex File
>
> He was Released Amidst Rape and Sexual Assault Allegations
>
> The professional was released today, weeks after being hired amidst rape allegations by a woman who claims he sexually assaulted her 4 times. The star denies the allegations but his employer decided to release him anyway.

It's political and business anymore, Bruh. Your employers aren't sticking up for you like that anymore. "Stand by your man" is over for many of these man-employer relations. Oh, they give the proverbials: "We released him so that he has time to clear his name,...": "He's not representing what we're about": "He doesn't represent our brand": and so on. But the truth is, your plight is bad for business or it is exceptionally good for business. Once again, they get to use an alleged perpetrator for drama – maybe people will watch their entertainment more and the drama may increase the season's ratings. Once again, they knew Mr. *Alleged* Perpetrator had issues before they brought him on. Weeks later you fire him? Why did you hire him?

Scandal is a money-maker publicity stunt that sensationalizes coverups and lies to sell shows, entertainment, politicians, books and personalities. Scandal dupes the public to believe what is half-truth, 1% truth or plain lies to make mo' money. Some of us love it; some of us are wising up to scandal advertising.

The danger of us buying lies and shit from the money-makers is, people can tell us any shit and we believe it. There's a point where the liars make you believe you're responsible for their shit. There is a point where lies are life and death for the public. Fear? Look around you. Look past what they present you and what they tell you. Each time they deliberately test us and feed us a half-truth and we buy it, they take note of that. The next time they feed us less truth and more lies; the more we believe, the more they realize they can bullshit us into anything. Welcome to yet another episode of The "Dumbing Down" of the Masses.

They got sponsors, Man. You're a liability. It doesn't matter how well you entertain, play, or make them money; nor what an asset you think you are. Leave the small pussies alone, Man. Stop sexing and playing with women (girls) who are playing you. They're not that into you. It doesn't matter how much power you think you have because you made the top of the ladder or the big leagues. It only takes a small pussy to take you out. You're bigger than that. You're a king. Stop playing with "commoners". "Commoners": small pussies intentionally sexing and playing men to take them out.

There's nothing common about you, Woman. Stop acting like that. You're a queen. Go get your own bank legitimately, if you're screwing him to take him out. That's bitch; you're Queen. That's extortion; that is criminal.

Man, know the rules and your rights, especially for the corporations and entities using you. Find one She that is into you. This is now. That old game of having who you want, when you want, how you want, because you're a star, is over. There is a sector of the She species that is out for you. She's playing like that – to take you out. If you sexed her (even once), it doesn't mean you own her. What the hell do you have to say for yourself, Man?

Get a fight if you have a right and stop letting people bully you, especially if you're innocent.

What IF

What if men say: "I sacrificed my life, my time and my family for this opportunity. This career is my life-long dream. I'm not leaving because *she* wants me to leave."

What if the law says, there is a statute of limitations for eyeballing a woman or man 20 years ago/a year ago and hanging them on the gallows.

What if men say: "These are my eyes, dammit, and I can look wherever the hell I want to look"

What if men say: "You're in my space, dammit! Don't bend your ass over in my space! Get the hell out of my space!"

What if?

In many cases it is imperative that the law addresses the intent and says you cannot be in his space like that.

Oh, discrimination!

What if men say: "You're discriminating against me by presenting your ass like that in my personal and immediate space? That is offensive to me and that is bothering me. I don't like it because it could cost me my job, my life, my company; so get it the hell out of my face: get it the hell out of my space!"

What if men say: "You're a liability to my company, Woman. I own this! Get out!"

What if men start suing women et al for defamation of character? What if men start suing women for their losses? What if men declare war on women? You know what? We've already hit "men" in the scrot and knocked the wind out of many of them.

Women: They've done it to us for thousands of years.

They have and that is wrong; address your thing. The fact that it has happened for thousands of years says women know a dick when they see one too. They know the game. Every woman is not taking advantage of the dicks. Every woman is not gaming. Many are. If you made a mistake and misjudged him, you can still walk away. Walk away from the dicks and forego the games, even if you can get $100K or a million. Don't be so impressed with Mr. Sexual Assault and Mr. Rapist that you stay in his circle (getting assaulted and raped, or not) because he owns a mansion, a car, an island or a nation. He's a rapist or a sex criminal. You report his ass. Get your SELF up and out of there! Take a stance, Women! A stance that you will not tolerate his shit because there is something in it for you. You don't need him to feed your love of nice things, your relentless pursuit of status, nor your deep insecurity to network with the players. These are some of our truths we have to face. As wrong as he is, we know better (most of us). Get your own things.

When the sexual justice arena becomes so vicious that hate spreads like pipedreams, we contaminate what may have been a good equitable cause with killer forces. Are we really ready for this war? Are we really ready for this war if men come back at women?

In a perfect world where all men could rise above their libido, you could pump your pussy in his face and he could still see your queen inside. The world is not perfect. The best of them can see Queen beyond the ass in his face. For others, that is just a pussy; you're just a pussy; he's really confused.

When women become more of a liability than an asset, no one

wants us on their books. Nobody likes liabilities that cost their life. Anyone has a right as the owner of a company, as a board, as an organization, as a system, to decide that this is costing me more than it's benefiting me – my organization, my company, my family. People can decide that this is destroying what my generations have lived, worked and fought for. Men can say, "We will not have liabilities on our hands in our company and in our corporation."

CHAPTER 30
BOTTOMLINES

Why aren't corporations and women being held accountable for not addressing sexual injustice cases when they happened? Women reiterate that their silence was rooted in fear of losing their jobs, their positions and what they had worked for. Where are healthy environments for women to say and the accused to be treated fairly? Where are the healthy environments that proactively train and retrain men and women?

Gender relations is apparently not an obvious skill.

Companies have systems in place that work to maintain and grow their money bottom-line. Many companies invest in career development. Some even support psychological health, rehabilitation and development. What about employees with relational issues (particularly gender relational issues)?

"Oh, that's their personal problem."

When their personal problem is in your company's workplace and in your bottom-line, maybe you should insist that he gets counseling, rehab or boot camp: send him packing or require mandatory rehab systemically designed to stop it. If he is that valuable to you, invest in systemic protocols to address sexual harassment and sexual crime-related issues and enforce them, or pay later. Systemic solutions should be a daily routine, especially given our epidemic gender relations crises.

If your star player who brings in 90% of your billion-dollar revenue has a problem, you get him help. The $50K fine he had to pay for saying the F-word the wrong time is trite. If it is your 1-percenter man who (you think) has a problem, you send him packing. Sorry, Small Fry, one-percenters are a dime a dozen. Go help yourself, Bud.

If we fail to realize that many men and women have killer issues with sexual relations, we will continue to fail at sexual relations in the workplace. And perhaps, if he is that out of control, he shouldn't be in the workplace. Perhaps he should be in rehab. The truth is, like any addict, the problem goes that deep for many people with sex crime/sexual issues. If we continue to ignore this or treat their issues lightly with means that are ineffective, we will continue to have the same results; and, our sexual divides will widen. We can leave the sex play as a weapon for the societies and powers-that-be to take a bastard down or we can annihilate it.

What is the context of our sexual harassment claims? What is the environment? We cannot foster and tolerate these environments for hundreds of years and get mad one day like two year olds and say, "I'm not playing anymore". The one holding all the cards to take him down and screaming the loudest is as guilty as everyone around the water cooler but she was just playing the game with them too.

CHAPTER 31
SMOKESCREENS AND COVERUPS

How much of our Sex War is a smokescreen or a coverup?

1.   Which Sex Files are smokescreens?
2.   Is his Sex File a coverup for something else?
3.   Find the fire. What's really behind the smoke? What is this really about?

There are corporations using the sexual misconduct thing to get rid of people. They use the sex drama of a Mr. Sexual Misconduct to cover up what is really happening or use Mr. Sexual Misconduct's sexual impropriety for their benefit – cater to sponsors' whims, create a sexual profiling advertisement buzz, serve the prevailing political genre or the society. This one is a Race File (so far) but many Sex Files follow the same scheme.

Race File

Today, this Show fired their new hiree (Mr. Slur) days after he was hired because he made racial slurs or used racially toned material directed towards a certain ethnic community (Ethnicity X) on his popular blog during his career. The Show claims they want to appeal to a variety of audiences and point of views.

Apparently, this high profile Show, who knows their business, did not know about Mr. Slur's racially-questionable material BEFORE they hired him.

It is incredulous that this Show did not know about their new hiree's racial slur(s). These are the scenarios that most of the critics of our movements, our media and our politics find biased, dishonest and wrong. Our ways and means of addressing "bad" people and practices are speculative, at least. Your public is reading what you do not say about the Show. The public is reading what the sexual justice movements do not say about the corporations and entities who fire Mr. Sexual Misconduct. They are reading between your lines about what you do not say about the sexual harassment or misconduct cases. They are at a loss to understand why a person's life is ruined when those ruining it did not act in all fairness to the party they destroyed: when those ruining it are more guilty.

1. Why would a "reputable" Show hire someone without vetting them properly?
2. Why should the world believe that a Show that knows their business does not know a (popular) new hiree enough to know if he represents their business or not?

This drama certainly looks like the Show is trying to appeal even more to Ethnicity X by publicly humiliating Mr. Slur: especially since Mr. Slur presumably dissed Ethnicity X with his slurs. Not only does using this scenario to attract more of Ethnicity X infer that the public is naïve about our sensationalistic marketing and advertising tactics that "create a buzz". It says to the world, it is okay to destroy someone to get what you want. (Of course, it is okay to destroy someone only if you are certain people; everybody else has to obey the law.)

Of course, popular media is pointing the populace (with all their might) to what the new hiree, Mr. Slur, did instead of what Mr. Corporation did. Of course, Mr. Corporation must stand by the reasons they give to secure their ratings, their popularity, their network's sponsors – political or other. It cannot be that they stand up for the new hiree instead of their underhanded tactics. Mr. Corporation cannot admit that anything they did is questionable or wrong. They cannot admit that they are using this new hiree for their benefit - publicity stunts/buzz, stellar ratings from their new audience en masse, whatever political games scheme behind the scenes.

When, in America, did someone in a career dedicated to "edgy" material lose his voice? Why does he not have a chance to walk the damn tight rope of "from-now-on" if that is what he wants to do? Especially in light of our newly found consciences, why didn't he get a warning? Or when did we all miss that it is not okay to talk about other races or to slur?

Coverups are as prevalent as our social issues. We use them for whatever suits our bottomlines. Where are we using race-related coverups to increase our audiences and our following? Where are we using sexual crimes coverups for our political advantage and other? Where are coverups using rap music for gang violence? The music is beautiful; the stories are powerful. But if we're using the platform to kill brothers and somehow "legitimize" gang activity, rap is a coverup. The rap (all that it embodies) is still fascinating, powerful and appealing; where is it a coverup?

When is it okay to say "certain" things – racial slurs and all - and when is it not? Who makes The Rules? Who informs the rest of the world? Are we all supposed to know that given a certain climate – sexual, political, or racial – we should not say and do certain things? Why isn't it always wrong to be racist? Why isn't it always wrong to sexually assault someone? WHY? Our shades of gray are suddenly in the black and Buddy (Mr. Sexual Misconduct), you'd better know it!

This is wrong. We must fix our ways, our systems and our actions. Particularly, those of us swaying popular opinion with only some of the facts. We are defrauding one another and getting away with it. If you hired your new hiree to use him to get a certain ethnic audience, why are you right and he is wrong?

Certainly an entity like the Show has better vetting processes to know that a person in such a career for over 10 years has had some "slurs". Who hasn't had "slurs"? Including Mr. Corporation's canners. It seems Mr. Corporation used Mr. Slur for their personal gain and tried to execute a kill the "bastard" on him and his career. Find another humane way to get your ethnic audience from Ethnicity X or to attract variety. To make the Show's agenda more emotive, they hired another new hiree from Ethnicity X at the same time that they fired American Mr. Slur. Certainly, if you keep the new hiree from Ethnicity X and get rid of Mr. Slur (the American), this looks even juicier to Ethnicity X: the ethnicity you're wooing. Oh, salacity!   How far will we take these foul practices? People, find another humane way to get what you want instead of using people. Was Mr. Slur wrong for saying what he said? Was Mr. Corporation wrong? Who defends Mr. Slur? Who?

Is Mr. Sexual Misconduct wrong? Again, this is not about right and wrong. That is settled. This is about very comprehensively looking at every possible aspect of this Sex Thing, of our race things, and being fair to all parties involve. This is about telling the truth about all of the story. Otherwise, we need to leave the Sex Thing until we are ready to be (i) HONEST and (ii) FAIR to everyone.

Sexual Misconduct may be a reason corporations give for firing people, but it is not always the real reason. Yes, he may have looked at her ass or groped her or other, but if you have some other beef with him, make sure you're not firing him for the other beef. Maybe the other beef has to do with the power plays behind corporations that are politically motivated. If indeed we want to go to the extent of calling this notion one of the twilight-zoney conspiracy theories that we scoff at, may the masses consider all of the factors.

Impetus

If we really tell everyone, "Our primary sponsors are left-winged and they will bow out if we keep Mr. Sexual Harassment", everyone will see the injustice in that. If we really tell the truth about why we are firing some of our Mr. Sexual Misconducts, the world will know that corporations are using the sex crisis as smokescreens and coverups. Certain actions by corporations are reputation killers for alleged Mr. Sexual Misconduct. With sponsors playing politics, corporations bottom-lines can take a hard hit if they ignore their sponsors' request to "get rid of him".

Oh, what a capitalist society we are! Our bottomlines and agendas are our gods and we play with double-edged swords. With one side some corporations appease their power-player sponsors and with the other, they have catered to their star man (although he may have had a sexual harassment tab as long as eternity). With the current Sex Crisis, the star man has to go these days. The star who was sexually harassing for many years now has to go.

Silence is condoning.

We cannot allow sexual harassers free reign (some for years) without condoning their behavior. The harassed should have a safe place to tell; corporations should have systems to resolve;

harassers should have the right places to go after comprehensive and fair consideration; alleged sexual offenders are alleged until all sides are presented to the right ears (not necessarily public opinion). Twenty years later, companies dump him for Sexual Misconduct when he pissed them off way before the heinous act. Company, House, Senate and all are not letting him go for sexual misconduct/crimes, but doesn't have the character to state that their agenda is bigger than that. In the name of the almighty dollar, corporations and personalities are getting rid of people. Of course, $20 Million severance bucks to a multi-billion dollar corporation is cheese compared to losing hundred-million-dollar sponsors.

CHAPTER 32
FOUNDATIONS

Corporations, Politicals, Hollywood, et al, if sexual harassment was prohibited for decades and you knew about Mr. Bastard and did nothing, what gives you the right to destroy Mr. Bastard today? Perpetrators, many of them still "alleged" perpetrators, are going down without recourse. We have these certain protocols to save our necks and bottomlines, or to serve our causes, while a woman is living in corporate hell (or hell) with sexual victimization. The bottom line? She was being victimized before sexual regulations and for thousands of years.

The curtain has fallen on an era where religiosity crucifies the bastard and the sinner alike. The religioso crucified bastards in pious self-righteousness back in the day when one of theirs "fell from grace". For some it wasn't pious self-righteousness but because they really believed it was the right thing to do. In light of religioso moving on from crucifying the bastards, institutions and groups have adopted the practice with vehement force, especially if it serves their politico, their agenda or their "self". We hang saint and sinner in the name of morals and morality and zero tolerance. (It is shocking that we have tolerance for some of the things some of the times. For an era of que sera tolerance, we sure have a stance on the Sex Crime thing: especially for certain people.)

Our newly found "morals, morality and zero tolerance" are in name only because the real reasons lurk in our desperate political agendas, schemes and evil so high up, we cannot find the raging fire. There is a reason for the burn. Where there is smoke (smokescreens) there is fire. The fires are massive and if we sniff the stink of the smoke, we can smell fear. It is a different scent than the other smokescreens. It is unfamiliar. It is unfamiliar because the top of the ranks are scared. It is the first time they've been this afraid. And so, as we go, the top guns pull out whatever stops to keep their power, maintain position, go higher or win. The stakes are high in their game – they play life and death games. Merciless power players they are. Anything goes, including slaughter - careers, political aspirations, life. We're not as bold as Hitler. We're more underhanded with our tactics, but accomplish our goals to destroy and annihilate.

There are opportunists that use the sex cause to get sexual justice for their causes.

There are unscrupulous people who use the sex cause to get whatever they want – their man in office, their piece of the oil slick money, their piece o' the money, their fleeting moment of fame, their ...

Many of the unscrupulous really don't give a flea about victims and their plight. If we did, we wouldn't have collaborated all of the big stories of sexual deviance for one moment in time. We would have addressed them ("big or small")when we learned about them, individual by individual, case by case: whether someone was listening or not: whether she was famous or no-name: whether our money was in her sex-trafficking nation or not. Most of the institutions, societies and power players that kept the masses silent on sex crimes are only allowing voice to the sex crisis agenda for their benefit.

There are wars in the ranks of societies, brotherhoods and power schemes. Behind the politicals and kingdoms, organizations, power families and big business play any card to rule the world: the world of bank. The politicals are fighting for power but that is all most of us see. The reds and blues really need a big play this time because so much is happening behind the scenes to threaten the power players. They must incite the masses to win this time. The victims are just an end to their means, pawns in the sex games: dirty rags. We are really trying to take down presidents, but there is even more to it than that.

In the name of political correctness, we are placing women in positions of power and slaying men. Woman Power is making deals with dirty boys in Fat Cat ranks in boys' clubs. In the name of money, we are destroying the innocent with the guilty. In the name of power, we are abusing the victims of sex crimes to jockey for position in societies and brotherhoods. What we build will only have the same composition. Society needs good men and women in leadership, but how we get there will determine our success or failure. Shitty has never bred greatness. Shitty can only breed shitty.

Why are so many women still supporting Mr. Sexual Offenses? It is not so much that women are supporting them or voting for what they did. A lot of women have an extreme hatred and disgust for the agenda of institutions (Bitches and Witches) whose only goal is to castrate men or serve their agenda. Some of us love our men more than the Bitches and Witches hate them. Some of them "love" their men.

Women aren't voting for the beautifully damned bastard who committed the atrocious. Women are voting against the destroyers whose only putrid agenda is to destroy, including men. Women who vote like that are not voting against victims. Most of them empathize with victims. Some of them are victims themselves. They vote to kill something they find more odious – The Bitch and Witch agenda.

Most women hate a bitch and a witch more than they hate a bastard – enough to slay a bitch or a witch with a vote. Know how to champion your cause and keep the bitches and witches out. You may win America and the world better on the sexual justice thing. Fix your causes or you may not get that vote. Where is resolve instead of castration? Instead of murder? Where is equity instead of hate? It is one thing to use the public venue to bring a power player to the table. It is another to be underhanded in our means to kill them. In the eyes of many, that is just as shitty as sexually harming someone. It is just a different context. Oh the satisfaction when you take his money, his work and his power. A bitch is never satisfied with this. There is a public who finds such salacious fare revolting to their core.

CHAPTER 33
IN THE SHADOWS

Sex is Economy. Hence the current racket to take out administrations. He who rules one of the most powerful stock markets in the world rules killer bank: that's power. Oh, and the ranks smell it like maggots smell stink cheese. The power shifted with the last political swing. The vicious and mad grab to take the reins back is a vicious and mad grab to take back one of the world's most powerful economies.

The losers of the political games rolled the tapes of the winners' sex bad to influence public opinion. Sexual Justice influencers (causes) still ride the wave of power player games or fuel the fire. Some influencers just want sexual justice. Others play the Big Boys' Clubs for favors and position. In a world of dirty fighting, most of us can't trust our hearts to agree or disagree with this statement: Much of our Sex Crisis passion is tainted. We've convinced ourselves that killing the bastards is pure and just and right.

What do we want?

Really.

What do we want?

Dirty hearts play dirty games. They cannot be satisfied. For even if we thought we got what we think we want, we will still want something else. It's okay to want. It is not okay to want, fight, steal and kill to get what is not yours to have. That equals greed. We are no different than the unconscionable regimes that steal food from bloated-belly starving children and let it rot. It's all greed. Be careful what lies beneath. Greed is greed – no matter how we package it.

Sex is power. Power has a responsibility. Power has responsibilities. Oh sex does its responsibilities, with pleasure, but we make our SELF house and senate over sex and mess it up.

It's fascinating that the sex tapes of the other side haven't surfaced. Oh, they're out there. The power player losers with the sex game in their hands will not play their own tapes.

It is unfair to ourselves not to consider that behind our greed, our illicit sex plays and our vices is something that is bigger than us.

There is a world behind the sex card more underhanded, sinister and deadly than we know. And, "No", this is not Conspiracy Theory No. 487. This is an age-old system playing itself out. Yes, your sexual fiasco fifty years ago when dirty sex was a norm is being used for a bigger picture.

All of a sudden, we feel the need to do the right thing and with such force, we are taking down the best of them (or the worst) without due course – System.

All of a sudden, in a nation of rights, the greatest of them have no rights – System.

When did one person pass judgement on another to destroy their life and career without due course? -System. When?

Why all of a sudden, can extremists swing an axe and slay whomever falls in its path? System.

What is worse than that, is the accused just complies without laying the dirty cards of their accusers on the table; some of the accused get an investigation or trial; some just walk with their one box of career murder under their armpit. Is he guilty? Maybe some. Are his accusers? Some.

Is it fair that the accused walks with his little white box under his armpit? Not while the filthy Big Boys Club of secret societies use his demise to orchestrate their strategy. Not while many of the women were in it for the money, status, position or power – prostitution. Not while many of the women accusing him were more than willing to sex him as a married man, therefore did not give a shit about his children, nor his wife, nor him.

Why is adultery okay? Why is it "legal"? It's definitely okay because the organizations, hashtags, politicos and media are not killing the bastard women. Why is it okay for her to play a role in destroying his home? His home was destroyed before their first innuendo because of their messed up heart places. Where is the law for women willing to play a married man? Why doesn't the media take up arms with the women having affairs and destroying homes the same way they scandalize his burn? Why don't we say a big "OMG" at her? Why aren't we as interested in the fact that she is F- ING a married man? What does that say about her? What does that say of her character? Of her scruples? Of her?

Where are the law, causes and the media for women deliberate and intentional on destroying a man? Where are the law, the causes and the media and for women deliberate and intentional on destroying a man because he confronts her? Bruh, if she will F you and you are married (with or without children), there is a strong possibility that she will try to F you. If she will F you and you have "nothing" with her, there is a good possibility she will try to F you.

Don't let up with your one box under your armpit if you have rights. Her ability to F a married man and game you begs the questions: What else has she done? Who else has she screwed? Why is she suddenly better or different than you? Her ability to F you on a one night stand or two week stand, begs the question, What else will she do to F you up? Maybe it's just an "innocent" one night stand. Is it? Given the current sexual crime wave, do you want to do that with her?

Men, watch out for set-ups. It is unfair to the accused when she had a consensual sex thing with him: when one of their sex plays got misconstrued or other. It is illegal and wrong when she was playing him for his money, status or favors – prostitution. The prevalent system of fear that silences an intelligent and accomplished man is inconceivable. We can only see this if we think outside of our boxes. This is a bigger picture one.

Oh! It is bigger than taking down presidents and political parties. Much bigger. The hate is vehement enough to go there (to the bigger picture), but ... will we go there?

There really are bigger pictures: good and bad ones. Some people call the bigger picture life, others the universe, some call it God, others karma. Sex is one of those things that nobody really owns. It's sort of its own entity. It has laws and rules. When we operate with sex from damned places (evil, darkness, underhandedness, etcetera), we are at the mercy of what our damned places produce.

"Why you hate The Bastard so much?"

Don't tell the world it is because we have a sudden conscience and passion for our sexually scourged souls. It is not our sudden Sexual Humanitarian mission. If we had such a passion for sexual abuse, we would have addressed it when She came to us bloody and raped in the heat of our trembling anger that declared, *"He* did this to you?!"

If we look at what we hate – presidents, Russia, personalities, money plays that threaten our bank, power games that do not include right wingers (or left wingers for the other side) - we could see the bigger picture better. It does not end here at these "petty" things. Follow the money, big money, and go very deep if you can stand the heat. There you will find the smoldering bigger picture: in the cauldrons of hell. If you dare go deeper, if you survive, you will find, the big picture. Fear is afraid that it is about to be exposed in a way that upsets the power systems of this world and shakes the world to the very core. The big boys are fighting. It's a kill fight.

Sex File: Big Boys Club

This "Power Player" died, alleged by suicide, in his prison cell. He was the associate of the leaders who play behind-the-scenes in institutions and societies.

Organizations, societies, boys clubs, girls clubs, and cultures have sex laws, covenants, oaths and belief systems. THEY still use these as tools to control, advance and scheme. We've been granted a freedom of sex that works by design and we choose, every day, to be bound by the sex terms of this society or that organization.

It is flabbergasting that people watch the demise of players in such organizations and still swear by them. Kingpin passes the scepter to the winner of the squabbling in the ranks or the winner of the squabble takes all; and the jokes of spades tote water for a place on the board of small people. You're a big people. Why are you toting water hoping to advance the ranks of Big Boys' Club?

The very dominance of this class or that class should tell us that something is wrong with the game. The fact that your daddy only got so far and his daddy only got to water-toter should tell us something.

"Well, they're still using Mother. That will get me to the top." He says.

You still insist that one day, "Momma is gonna rise!" Where was Grandmomma when she left?

You're it - Kingpin, Ace or Queen. You don't have to dance to the societies that use the sex to control, manipulate and destroy you. That is what the system does. When the sex designer gave you sex freedom, why are you branding your thighs and your heart to a society or cult game you will never win?

"I want to be The King."

"I want to be the Queen."

Ohhh! You want to be The Queen.

Do you know the cost of being The Queen? Do you know what price she is paying to be that? They own her. The societies, orgs and girls clubs own her. They barter like this: your soul for rank. Unfortunately, you don't even have anything they want, except your head or shoulders for them to walk on. What have they done for you? While you struggle to buy $5 gas for your clunker, the queens are buying lipstick for $100. Help a sister out.

You still want to be Queen?

You are.

CHAPTER 34
CLEAN UP YOUR RANKS

If we dig into the first power player that bit the dust, we would see that the game behind his demise was deliberate. How does a big fish play so long and suddenly become a target? Yes, it was a political move and maybe he pissed off one of the bigger fish, but power players don't just make moves like that. The feeding frenzy is at the top of the club.

Do they bring down another sex predator badass to take down their target and win the fight to rule a nation and the way its money plays? Watch the organizations, societies, cliques and "good old boys clubs". The main players are in a battle among themselves. Within the ranks of evil, blackmail is just one of the tools to silence and control. The sex game stage is contaminated. The players have their own rules. Again, the playing field is rigged. Again, injustice to the masses is a viable option.   Victims nor predators will come to a stage where they will be crucified, abused, used and misjudged. Clean up the stage!

Not to minimize any of our stories, but there is a lot of shit in the closets of the people who started this game. Stink shit. And, yes, they don't care who they use to stay undercover, including the victims of sexual harassment. Like every other game, Honey, you're just a ploy. Tell our victimization stories or keep them to ourselves. The picture is bigger than all of us. Even the feeders at the top of the totem pole must answer to the main players.

Our causes are noble. Our means questionable (at least). It is important to take a stand, but:

1. Check your real motives for your stances. Check their motives for using your cause. How politically motivated are they? Politics isn't just politics. Politics is about who controls the money and other power plays. It is about how the money moves and to where.
2. Why is there a sacrificial lamb? There needn't be a lamb if we act with tact. The one person being treated unfairly in our moments of great sex crimes epiphany is a victim. We take down a person with political murder and career murder when we draw the line across their shine: their time in history.

We could have said "From now on, this law will be enforced or that is fair." When the top guns in the societies were allowing the collective Mr. Bastard to get away with sex crimes for decades, they said, "You are allowed to be a lawless bastard. You are allowed to intimidate a subordinate with sexual (and other) innuendos." Now the top guns are saying, "We have a political hopeful we despise, so you (lawless bastard who we knew about for decades) have to go down to establish this sex crime stage to kill this potential political contender that we must not allow to get into office."

The office of president isn't really about the office. It's about the money, the power and who owns the pie. We're slaughtering people, especially powerful men, on a lot of subjective stances that don't fly in the arenas of total fairness. Total fairness requires painstaking inspections into all aspects of the Sex Crime case at hand, including how the Big Boys Clubs are using the victim's case for their means.

Sex File

Today, he is dead before he could stand trial. He was the associate of leaders, royalty and money players.

CAUSE OF DEATH: "Suicide".

There is no autopsy yet but they tell us: he killed himself. They direct the media to tell us about his extracurricular activities too: an unbearably heavy sex rap sheet.

All of this plays out on the public stage to take the eyes of the world off his high-ranking associates. Once again, the world only follows the part of the story they want us to follow. A big fish is dead: not surprising. That is how the societies and clubs play their games. Today you may be in. Tomorrow? Out or dead.

Who really killed him? Surely a man with leaders and prominence in his circles of associates had better keepers. Surely he had more hope to get off with such connections. Maybe he was their sacrificial lamb. (There are many sacrificial lambs these days: from the families of wealth and prominence to the societies of cults. Rappers don't just die and American Royalty isn't just cursed.) Maybe his Black Book was too telling and implicated the ranks in the Top Feeders' circles.

As a public it is one thing to be naïve, it is another to be suspicious; it is vital to require good from the heads that rule over us. It is wrong to kill Mr. Working Class Sexual Harassment while Mr. Power Player Sex Trafficker sucks caviar in swank. We started this Sex War with one king pin but the ranks are playing filthy games. The consequences are more severe for power players who kill bastards and blame it on the current public voice (the demands of the sexual justice organizations, hashtags, leaders and social sects). These power players live worse than the bastards they kill – hypocrite is so nice. What are we doing? We must wake up to see what is really happening.

It is critical that we wise up to what is really happening in our world. Once again, the players have tricked the masses into a stupor of a fraction-of-half-truths about The Sex Crisis. What is really going on? It is aching how powers-that-be test the masses and dupe the masses to see what else we will just buy (believe) at face value. Hitler sold his shit story to an entire nation and many of them bought his bullshit before they realized that he really was killing innocent people and children.

Before you comment about the next small fry or high rank that falls prey to our sudden Sex Crisis conscience, find out what is really going on. And if we are really true to ourselves, if he goes down, it's time to play the black books. If we are not being fair to all of the people, we need to sit down and shut up. Why does the law only apply to poor working class or a certain ranking Joe Blo? Why doesn't the law apply to the ranks? There is a severe price for this – a price we cannot pay. It is critical that we (our organizations, our groups, our hashtags, our ranks) fix this or go back to the drawing board before we perpetrate our agendas on another person's life – fire another Joe Blo, kill another ranking Aficionado or demand the resignation of another senator or politico.

Top feeders sit in high-and-mighty places talking about keeping their putrid circles in place to preserve the greater good when the kingdom is in ruins. The core is a defecation of disease and we're trying to preserve the greater good. All we're trying to preserve is defecation. Clean up! When we're ready to clean up from the top down and from inside out, we have a chance of building "greatness". Otherwise, it's just another show, and sweating with all of our might to build more shit on defecation. Sooner or later, the world will be privy to this. And people will insist on equity in the ranks of boardrooms and power players before they walk the plank because dirty Power Player said so; because hashtag said so; because media or she said so. That's called a revolt. Clean up your ranks.

CHAPTER 35
THE VOTE

Sex File

Why did over 60% of white women vote for Mr. Alleged Sexman after his sex story rocked the world? Why did almost 50% of voters still vote for him? With multiple sex allegations (some over 40 years old), why did he still have nearly 50% of the vote? As loyal as people are to their racial side and political side, why isn't the sex card swaying Mr. Alleged Sexman's state that much? Mr. Alleged Sexman hung from the sex politics lynch with blazing fire under his boots, hazardous fumes in his nostrils and a filthy noose around his neck, but almost half of voters still chose him.

POINT: We practically raised the dead on this one with alleged sex crimes over 40 years old.

POINT: There are parental roles in the cases of Mr. Sex with a Minor.

POINT: There is the role of teenager in the case of Mr. Sex with a Minor.

Yes, Mr. Sex with a Minor is wrong but the other facts are. It sounds really raw but if we face the facts, we may strategize better for the next political soiree or we may make some progress on resolving our sex and gender issues.

In "Comprehensively Speaking: The Vote":

1. Women and voters may have been considering the whole story. 2. Women and voters know our agendas can be filthy and vindictive. People hate that. 3. "Christian" labels Christians with an ability to forgive (not condone perpetrators, not to discredit the abused, nor to trivialize a victim). When the unforgiveable and unpardonable sin is forty years old, infected with the stench of every agenda of the current sex climate and we're only telling a part of the story, the juries of public opinion think twice about slaughtering an accused offender.

The polls show that most people did not vote for Mr. Alleged Sexman.

1. Race has a strong tendency to stick together. If the powers-that-be in your race demographic say Mr. Blue is the man and your race needs the powers-that-be to get where they're going, they're going to vote for Mr. Blue.
2. Races have a strong inclination to blue or red in certain states.
3. Racial issues don't just die.

When you can't take down a power player because he's too high up the food chain, you take down the house from the bottom up. So we find the vice that will destroy him and start attacking everyone with the same vice who has a certain dollar sign on their money game or a certain position: a position we want for ourselves or for someone who will benefit our bank. We try to take him down to place someone in power who will benefit our power or our position.

The sexual harassment/sexual crime vice isn't just about the women and victimized men and children. It is also a contraption for big fish. It is one of the ways the societies and Big Boys Clubs control one another and the power game. The problem is, the best basis for sinking a big fish is having significant grounds to sink him. The consensus is, if everyone else with his vice goes down, he must go down: if enough of the feeders on the bottom of the totem pole fall, the power player will go down for the same.

Whether Mr. Alleged Sexman goes down or not, it's time to look behind the scenes at the motives of the main players. It's time to make progress with our agendas that changes the world for better instead of just being vindictive if that is our motive. It's fair to look at the whole story.

CHAPTER 36
WHERE LEGENDS FALL

Today we watched a legend crash gracefully. As overwhelming as the "death" of a political figure that we only saw in part, the flippant killing of a dream is so far beneath us. In part, this legend was passionate because he loved the people he served. In part, his passion was a flame. The flame we call great politics is dimmer, less passionate, because the current sex crisis agenda was the catalyst that made him decide to exit the stage of politics. Most devastating is, it was pressure from his colleagues that contributed to his demise. It is fascinating that they didn't stand up for him. Instead they stood up for "the establishment". And so we do: "sacrifice one for the greater good", we call it. Truth? Fix the problem.

It is doubtful that this senator took the decision to take a bow from politics lightly. Some legends never die, no matter how they take a bow. No doubt, there are other flames for him to fan, more journeys to take and the scapegoat *has* triumphed. So, may he go forth into greater endeavors and accomplishments. We cannot destroy true greatness. There is always a bigger stage and in the end, the "greater good" pays a costly price because we cannot build success on injustice. Eventually, truth triumphs.

Do not take lightly the pen of power you hold. Do not use your sword of a leader's scepter to kill and destroy; for then, you are the instrument of a more hellish power. The way this hellish power plays is to eat even its instruments. In other words, your time will come. Justice is justice. Justice contaminated with other is not justice at all. Rotten-to-the-core has a tendency to rot anything it touches.

Whatever your claims and the claims of his victims, there is a beauty and a grace that does not die from mere injustice. Such beauty and grace defy the inequitable pen. They have a power of their own. They stand: even in the face of injustice. And even the weakest of hearts see what they do not know – weakness has no ability to fathom strength, darkness cannot comprehend light, injustice inevitably fails. As important as our stories of sexual impropriety are, they are buried when we sling them carelessly at the wrongly accused. In the halls of power players where he made a difference, true greatness takes a debilitating blow for the team.

The greatest sometimes shine where no one sees or looks.

Once again, the victim is diminished because a greater injustice is perpetrated on the accused: not the guilty: the accused. Once again, our stories are tainted with injustice. The victim is once again victimized. This time, it is the cause tainted that shoot holes in the victims' stories. The motive that is rotten-to-the core robs the real victim of her power.

Our stories and causes steal the victims' power when we contaminate them with kill-the-bastard mentalities, mindsets and intentions that are rooted in filthy places. If you get pleasure watching him or her squirm, check your humanity levels. We're in the red zone of sub-human universes that eventually eat us up. Once again, we sow seeds for our sons and daughters. It is unfathomable the price they have to pay for our sadistic.

CHAPTER 37
ANGRY PLACES

The anger runs deep for so many. And even when we come up for air to tell a story of bad sex, it has to be palatable for an audience unfamiliar with a soul that comes from sex hell. Some victims don't even know (technically) where the anger comes from. It is one thing to be angry (at something or someone). It is another to just be angry. Some of our anger is generations of fury. Sex anger gets piled in with other anger – our father, the slave boat from Africa, the injustices of our mother and her men, the struggles of whatever our battles. We are angry at him, at them, and if we look really closely, we are angry at ourselves.

Many of us don't really know this – that we are angry at ourselves – because it is easier to be angry at him, at them; and to some of us, we did nothing wrong. We happened to be there.

Angry at him can be normal; so is angry at them – the missing guardians (or parents), the societies, the cultures.

Victims can be angry at them because they didn't see, they didn't look, they didn't care, or didn't do. It is dungeon-like to be in a bad sex place or come from there. It is excruciating when they don't see nor hear the victim: even when victims don't say. Many women carry rape like toil in their bosoms. Some men have rape and sodomy stories that words cannot tell.

The people around us are supposed to see or hear such unspeakable things. They're supposed to take these things into account when they are "Judging Sex". But, victims learn to hide it so well. It is more unforgiveable when they knew and did nothing. Some wear the knowing like guilt. Whether it is as blatant as our bling or as subtle as khaki chinos, knowing affects us. Sometimes the affect is more subconscious. It affects.

We know how to live something of a life. We learn what makes us angry. Some victims try to avoid; some try to confront; others try to deal. But, one day some victims realize that they are angry. Anger is fuel, passion, drive. We may call it "making lemonade out of lemons" or "turning a negative into a positive". We may call it fuel, energy or drive, but we use it for something good. To use it is power. To place it is wise. To figure it out, heal and conquer it, is free.

Free has a different power than angry power. Angry power can build a career, take us up some corporate ladders or even make us billion-dollar networths. Free is the art of living copiously. (Not necessarily lavishly). Living free is true success. Until we arrive there – the art of living copiously or true success - something else fuels our pursuits, endeavors and accomplishments. Some days, even the angry places are inadequate. If the victim does not fight the quagmires of depression, anxiety and other fears, their sex file can swallow them up.

Most of us find a way to rally up ourselves (pull ourselves together to continue the fight: pump up). The rally gets old.

CHAPTER 38
PERPETRATORS

Perpetrators have the power to choose - to perpetrate or not - unless they give that power away to the ghosts that taunt them.

There are perpetrators that can be rehabilitated. We rehab every other human ill. They should be rehabilitated. Again, if a child learns sexual deviances, they learn other sexual norms. Things get in our hearts by some indelible event, by what we choose to feed on, by the mental mind thoughts we nurture and nourish. Some things are coded by our family tree – DNA.

It takes deliberate and constant efforts to retrain the brain, the heart, the mind. In many cases, this is not enough. It is deliberate to know the triggers. It is mandatory to stay away from it even if it only resembles temptation. Oh, we're not dealing with just 6-foot runway legs and luscious nubile lips temptations! Perpetrators' temptation games are with the other-force attractions that know their weaknesses. Run! Run the other way until you are free. Even when you are free, beware.

"That's no way to live."

There's always the other way – it's usually less desirable.

There are perpetrators who have crossed the line from human to demons. We cannot rehabilitate demons.

Some perpetrators choose to perpetrate. Why? Bitterness is a burden, a poisonous burden. Anger is necessary but using it to victimize is criminal. If perpetrators are angry at the beast behind their eyes, we can be more effective with the beast. If victims and sexual justice advocates are just trying to kill him or her for what he or she did, the deed lives on to breed more.

Yes. It's not your job to heal the world. We are as we are. If a victim's life is still affected by it in any way, it still has power over him or her. If you have to pretend you're okay, you're not okay. And sometimes we have to pretend until we can walk.

In classifying perpetrators, like degrees of murder, we have certain degrees of sexual bad. There are women perpetrators as well as men. Comprehensively speaking, we've sometimes missed the fact that women harass men too. Comprehensively speaking, we have inadequately classified women who sexually harass men. Perhaps it's because men have yet to bring this to the table.

In *"Checking Out His Ass"*, sexual advances by women come to light and there are millions of sexual overtures, tones and misconduct by women towards men and women.

The walls between the sex perpetrator and the victim only allow them to live from limited, superficial places; deeper places have a tinge of unknown to them. Unknown causes uncertainty. For victims and perpetrators, being close to anyone got associated with a bad sex event or a sexual encounter, so now closeness with anything carries a certain "thing". That thing was there – in the closets, in the secrets, in the dark, in the taboos: a ghost of sex.

The ghost of sex past is a haunting that lurks everywhere and in every relationship of victims and perpetrators if it is not obliterated. If you ever walked there – in the sex places – you get marked. Even the professional relationships and casual encounters have a sense of sex ghosts. That is, in part, why sexual harassment and sex themes are at work, in corporate walls, government halls and a part of organizations. People do not see people clearly with a sex ghost veiling their daily encounters. Who cares? What difference does it make if we see him or her clearly? Who cares how they see us? To the haunted and the gray-area-dwellers, all things are tinged with a haze. To the sex ghost-haunted among us, the same is true; all things are viewed with sex ghost-tinged glasses, consciously or subconsciously.

To societies, organizations, orders, people and other perpetrators: When you mark a person with sex scars, you mark them with a sex vulnerability that places them at the mercy of those who prey on such weaknesses. Whether we realize it or admit it, sexual abuse and encounters are a calculated and intentional scheme to direct the life of a victim to sexual deviance. To those who use sexual control for their benefit, they have a vice to control and take advantage of victims of sexual abuse and sexual deviances. To those who use sexual control for their benefit and to hurt another person, that is criminal.

We do not own nor control society. We can only control ourselves. Some of us, many of us, are challenged to do that. The triggers are. Someone will always remind you of back there. Something will always be sex nostalgia. Be deliberate about defying it. Say no to it. Find something greater than the bad sex that was. Live something bigger. Steer clear of the triggers. The other side (which is prevalent) is to indulge the old, the residuals from the old bad sex plays; hence, our current status quos, hashtags, stigmas, cultures and headlines. Finding something greater isn't necessarily a cure for the bad sex places; something greater may be a crutch but it can help us limp to places of overcoming the bad sex places or to places of healing eventually.

As repulsive as we find the predator who continues in the bad sex genre, victims can live limited lives when they choose to live from bad sex places. Instead of digging up the bestiality, incest, unhealthy heterosexuality, homosexuality, infidelities and affairs to find out why we sex that way and regroup, we create our own norms from these places.

"How dare we compare any of these sex lifestyles with sexual harassment, sexual abuse and sexual infidelities?"

"It is not a comparison."

Look at your thing in truth – whatever it is. Look at it in real truth, not your truth.

Incest isn't really about the fact that you sex your mother or your sister or your brother. Homosexuality is bigger than him sexing him or her sexing her. It is about you. Why are you humping a dog? What is it about your "sex" extreme? What is behind our sex things?   The great and flawless manufacturer of the sex is crazy about you. The great and flawless sex creator is into sex. He is into why it affects you so and why she settles when she is really a queen. He is into why a king does not know his domain. Sometimes King Man does not know how to sex her the way he's supposed to sex a queen.

CHAPTER 39
RAPE

They take a piece of you that you did not offer, that you did not give. Sometimes they take all. You lose it all or enough of you for the rape to cripple you ... Something in you dies. For that time, you die. Most victims wake up, the walking dead. Most victims only recover so much. Some do not recover. Others recover all.

The scars are sometimes infertility, sexual dysfunction, and reproductive disorders. The scars are sometimes predator scars that perpetrate bad sex stories on another. The scars are invisible. Invisible scars have a different kind of power. Because sex is so connected to the fountain of life and the vibrancy of life, many victims lose their life. We do not like to read nor hear stories like these. Like the starving and impoverished child on our TV screen, we switch the channel. We need to walk through stories like these if we are to be more effective: not just with rape: with our own sex causes.

Sex File

She pleaded with him. She begged. She begged him not to rape her.

"No, no, no."

As powerful as her words were, he could not hear. Before he raped her, even while he premeditated it, he had a chance to kill the mental torture in his head. Her No's were muted for he was driven by a power stronger than her pleas. The power in his own heart was more sinister, more demonic – venomous hate.

"No" came from her pleading. "Stop" came from her heart. The fear hit her because he persisted. "No no no" had a tinge of fear, of crying out, but she knew that fear meant to fight too. So she fought. He fought too. She fought and screamed with all of her life.

"NO!" "NO!" "NO!"

Whether her "NO!" was beaten with another fist that sent her heart reeling, or a fist to her face that turned her tears to blood, her NO was stronger. She fought harder but her fight inflamed him more. He fought back, but all in her was fight. Her fight only made his demons more vehement. He loved the challenge of the fight, the violence, the resistance: its power. In his sex files where a fight was an impassioned flame, he was incited to passion extremes.

Her fight was no match for his hate so fierce, yet she fought. He struck her and fought her to weaken and overpower her. He enraged her! She was beaten, but enraged. He fought her until he won. Hate had won. He had overpowered her, but her hate was even more than his demons. Inflamed with Hatred, he raped her. Inflamed, she lost it all where she died. She died because he took her life from her. It was poisoned with hatred. Repulsion scarred her life force.

He was vehement with his demons, psychotic in his soul; he overcame her. He hated her more. His demons drank her hatred like poisonous wine. In hatred, he rejected her. He left her there, repulsed, bleeding: bleeding repulsion: bleeding death. She ran away screaming the death of her soul. Her only refuge was in a place where she died. She stayed there.

She is only one of many of them, but all of their stories are different. Huriya was different because she was just a child. There are so many stories of child rape. If you can consider a nine-year-old girl covered in her raw filthy captors, drawing her last breath ... Perhaps, Huriya's hands reached out for someone to save her. Maybe, her hands were already limp and dead. And, maybe "dead" is about being "unsung", poor and culturally marginalized too. There was no one to help her. In a world of over seven billion people, not one person could help "Huriya". Where are we?

Power-players, you do not deserve your power, if you cannot help the Huriya(s) and the victims! If her voice is silenced, what did she live for? If her voice is silenced, what do you lead for? Why did Huriya die? We don't get to sit silently by. It is not so much that we tell the story. Do we tell it in pain, in anger, or maliciously? It is imperative that we change the course of the human race for good. And, if Huriya is too far from your doorstep, when you look into your granddaughter's eyes, when you look into your daughter's eyes, think of Huriya: occasionally, or until you spend yourself fixing the systems for another Syrian girl, Thai girl, Mexican girl, African girl, Russian or American: for another girl: another boy. Consider that there are millions of little girls and boys just like your Leila, your Jack, who deserve a chance at a beautiful life, just like them. And consider what your sex file is teaching Leila, Jack, Huriya.

CHAPTER 40
PICTURES

If you ever saw a picture of hate, you would believe in otherworldly. If you ever saw a picture of hate, you would know love when you saw it.

Her rapist could not force her if he loved her. Especially since she entreated him to stop and pleaded with him and begged him. Love is entreatable. If you speak with it (entreat it), it easily obliges anything that is good, that is truth. Only a thief takes. We lose our humanity where we take what is not ours. The danger of losing one's humanity, is that we become less than human. We are capable of the heart of beasts: beasts at barbaric levels. When we lose in us what makes us human, we've digressed to what is less than human: what is sub-human: what is inhumane.

We must confront and stop the hate that brings a human soul to such hell places. We cannot apply human means to forces that are otherworldly and expect for them to comply. We "put down" a dog that suddenly attacks its owner or a child. Perhaps, it is in fear that they have lost touch with our present reality, or perhaps, they will connect to the "former" beast in them and kill or hurt again. It is imperative that we can tell the difference between a serial rapist, the ones who feed on demons and those who are otherwise.

How does one lose their humanity like this? What lies does he (the rapist) tell himself? What lies does she speak to herself? Where are the places that one frequents to walk away with so many lies that he loses touch with his soul? A domiciled animal has limits and most never return to the creatures of the wild that they may have come from. How then, does a human being ever become so vile?

Crimes of passion, as they are nicely called, takes the human person from the ability to control himself to out of control: (if they ever were in control). Here, whatever passion controls him: not his human self. Does he hate because she refused him? Has he not learned to respond to "No"? Did he not learn that? The child who does not learn the game of their wider society in a home where the world sits at his or her feet, clash in a world that does not cater to their whim. Should society spare him or her because they are controlled by other? That is not what is implied here. Law and Order is wise to elevate rape cases to other levels that are effective with perpetrators who may be influenced by demons, ghosts or whatever foe.

Spoken sincerely, "I am sorry", bears within three words a power to heal, repair or extend a gesture that can change the game for victims. To some victims of rape, they mean nothing at all. Some victims may be validated that they are heard, respected and significant. Sometimes perpetrators can see, humble themselves and change; some perpetrators never change.

"I am sorry" from a place of *knowing* has a power to take the shame and all of its toxins away. This level of forgiveness is rooted in the persistence of women who demand their lives back. The raped victim repulses the rapist. The rapist in return rejects his victim. Herein lies rejection and repulsion in very profound ways. Repulsion is its own fierce force entity. Rejection is a power. They can take on a life of their own.

Don't let people hold you to those forces! Do not accept them. It may take time, but heal yourself or find healing in good safe places.

Live Beauty! Live! May you find in you, somewhere, the power to live!

CAVEAT

No one deserves to be raped.

It is commonplace to say this to rape victims – "You do not deserve this" or "You did nothing wrong to deserve this." So many rape victims need to hear this. There is nothing a woman can wear, do, nor say to make her deserving of rape. There is nothing a man can do that makes him DESERVE rape.

To some rape victims, it may be an insult to imply that anyone could possibly believe they deserve rape. But, the very definition of human defies the implications that anyone is deserving of rape or any other malady or injustice. We need to see this: The fact that we need to say such things – "You do not deserve to be raped" - defines how far we have come away from being human.

CHAPTER 41
INALIENABLE

Human endows us with inalienable intrinsic value.

Inalienable: rights that cannot be taken away.

Human guarantees us inalienable. People try to take our rights every day. It is one thing for them to take our rights. It is another for us to give our rights away.

We give our rights away every day when we trade our rights for favors. We cannot give up our sex, our equality and our power for a movie role, a step up the ladder, money, a man, a phone X and keep our rights. We live in a world where the opportunist waits: the lover waits too. We reduce ourselves to less than when we give up our inalienable. Hence the raw kill fight to get it back. We are so chagrined with fury to take back what we gave away, we are fighting dirty. You gave that up.

Opportunist is opportunist. Society is society. They wait for an opportunity to have your rights like waiting for a buzzing mosquito to land or just hover. Oh, the opportunists love it when you give up your rights. They will tear you to pieces. So we fight to get back basic human rights. So, we have to tell a human being they don't deserve rape because we've been programmed to think we deserve shit because we gave something up. It's not so much about deserve as it is about the fact that an opportunist will be an opportunist. They take advantage; that is what they do. We become more of an "easy" prey when we give up what is inalienable to us.

Just by definition of human, we deserve love, beauty, good, prosperity. These fundamentals are lost in our systems that treat us like slaves and victims of their imperfections. Part of our problem is we have not separated human from beast. Part of our problem is we stay in the vicious cycle of them. We treat human beings like animals – starvation, sexual crimes, injustice, corruption, systemic decrepit. Then we try to treat the maladies in our defective human codes with normal human means that are ineffective.

A rapist is governed by other forces. How did he get there? Is he ever capable of self-control? Does he ever own himself? We have to take that into consideration when dealing with him/her. We have to determine that. If we get the fundamentals right, we have good foundations to build something that is equitable to all of us. A sex trafficker: a bigot: a racist: a politically corrupt leader: scheming big boys in the big boys clubs: serial criminals and sexual harassers: societies and organizations that propagate evil: et al are governed by other forces. Once again, we've come so far away from the image of God that we are, we have to state the obvious. That is one of the problems with our ways.

Everyone is not capable of dealing with our "freedoms". He is flawed. He takes the "freedoms" so far out of context, he is not governed by anything but him-SELF or his demons: the defective way he thinks, his libido he does not care to control and his god. Do we subject ourselves to him and his skew by inhibiting our "freedoms"? We live aware of the abusers of our "freedoms", but we must consider if we have forfeited our true freedom with our compromises. We've compromised human for things. We've enforced systems that serve SELFISH. We've worshipped the money players because they have more bank. In so doing, we've reduced ourselves to lesser than. We can retrain or rehabilitate Mr. Skew, if we wish. As long as we have deviants in our societies, we must be alert and aware of that while we live the shades of gray.

Be wise women. Everyone should not be in your space. Who's your date? What are your parameters? Who's in your space? This is in no way blaming women for rape. This is not saying you deserve rape or any other injustice. Separate what is being said from what they tout and what you want to believe. Be deliberate about your space, who is in it and what they are there for.

She died from shame – right there where he raped her. She never recovered.

Sex shame holds us in some way. A rapist defies conscience if he persists. Justifying himself by whatever belief does not make him right. It is no different than normalizing shit. To continue sexual behaviors that are unconscionable to others numbs the conscience even more. Unconscionable defies the conscience. The conscience is that part of us that still holds us to be humanity. If and when we shake that off from holding us, we lose some part of our humanity: possibly all.

CHAPTER 42
COMPATIBILITY

To lose our humanity is to digress to what is inhuman: inhumane. Some of our repeated behaviors are an attempt to normalize the unconscionable (fight our humane). To do this, it is necessary to "blow off" what we do that is so unconscionable. What you make okay for you is not okay for her. Muzzling him like a dog with chains on his spread-apart ankles and locked wrists may be your norm, but what is the limit? It is vital that we understand that we all come from somewhere else, especially if We Ain' Family. Part of meeting people and dating is learning what we are, where we are from and if what we are will fly with him or her. Are you compatible? In every way? In the ways that matter most to you? To him or to her?

Compatibility is so much more than sexual compatibility. This is bigger than he likes jam; she like jelly. You can buy jam and jelly at the store. What really matters to you? To her? To him? If you don't know yourself, you will not really know what matters to you. Discovering oneself or each other after the fact is usually not the best relationship route. Some of us can work it out: some cannot. Lay your cards on the table before: all of them (especially if it matters to him: to her). *That* will come up if it matters: sometimes even if it doesn't matter: sometimes eventually. *That* – everything.

The fear that hides it because you are afraid he will not want you is an aspect of Papa Fear that will be the root of what destroys later. If you had a promiscuity problem and learned to be a prude, fix yourself. If you had a promiscuity problem and learned to cross the "sex" lines, adjust (especially, if your promiscuity extremes are too over the top for her): adjust or find another lover your equal.

The best common ground is love. Love is not our idea of love, our sex culture, our promiscuity. Love is not your prude. Love loves beautiful sexy love and sex like Chapter 1. Get yourself there. If you don't have that common ground, you will end up on his side, her side or some other side. And you will produce children like that - like you, one of you, another extreme or other. Then they meet someone else's child and spread the wealth of "unwholesome" sex culture. If that sounds like fear and negativity, look around at us – that's reality.

We talk about love being unbiased. We claim that love accepts all and love loves all, but love has ways, rules and laws that work for the best of humanity. Love says, "I love with my all. That is why I hate that": that which kills you. Love says I love you with all, but I hate what you're doing because it is killing you.

So we have what we have. If we do not get back to Chapter 1, we will self-destruct our own selves – no outer powers, other worldly force, second coming (if you believe or not). *We* – the collective human race that chooses to continue as they are - will self-destruct (whether we involve "mother nature" or not with our human nature). Self-destruct by yourself if you must. Leave people's children/loved ones/family alone. Inside the self is the human nature that tends to self-destruct. Inside is also the superior nature that tends to the good life. When we allow the human nature that tends to self-destruct to beat our pulse, it will destroy us. You

have no power over that beast: none. Inside the self is the image
and likeness of Lover. Let that beat your pulse.

CHAPTER 43
BROUGHT-UP-CY

Caveat: Most of us have the power to defy our brought-up-cy.

Sex Culture

You want to raise killers? Bring them up in the mafia.

You want to raise drug dealers? Bring them up in the drug trade.

You want to raise sex offenders? Bring them up in extremist promiscuity.

You want to raise white collar embezzlers? Bring them up in that society.

You want to raise good citizens? Bring them up in love.

We all have brought-up-cy. [Brought-up-cy: the way we are brought up or raised]. Most of us who escaped our bad brought-up-cy, only did because of the grace of God; not that the grace isn't there for those of us who are stuck there – we have to choose the grace over the bent; most of the times we need help doing this.

If a child learns promiscuity, they will be promiscuous: unless directed otherwise by some other directives. If a child learns sex shame, he or she will be sex shame unless retaught. If a child learns to be a prude, he or she will learn to be a prude unless he or she is re-cultured. If a child learns to sex, he or she will sex unless he or she learns and does otherwise. However and whatever he or she learned will be, unless he or she chooses Other. Depending on what we learned our sex norms are different; some are twisted, some are destructive, some are deadly. Eventually, some of us invite someone else to our sex culture and expect for them to play. Sadly, our sex culture pervades our life and spreads to our world.

When we expose our children to sex early, they learn sex through a child's mind. When we expose our children to bad sex early, we expose them to the world of bad sex. Most likely, they will have a proclivity to bad sex. They are trained to bad sex norms. Sexing has a tendency to expose the mind and heart to the cultures of good, bad, ugly or whatever energy or place – this world or other. There are other forces that are rampant in many environments where bad sex happens. Children and people get exposed to these other forces and other-worldly entities. They must contend with them; some must contend for the rest of their lives; some die in these hell holes. Many children escape the childhood sex trauma to arrive some place good.

A three-year-old is less responsible with sex than he or she is with racing a 2400 cc super hybrid power motorbike on the Autobahn at 300 km/h (186 mph). Not to mention their bodies are not built to handle either. There are certainly some physical limitations and detriment. The mental, psychological and spiritual ramifications of bad sex are afflictions to the human race for which we have no cure.

Many people grew up in very bad sex cultures. For those who had a "normal" childhood with no sexuality and promiscuity, please at least hear this – people who grew up in bad sex cultures did not grow up "normal". The ways from their culture as children were not like "normal" childhood children. Many children did not learn love. Many children learned some sort of sexuality, promiscuity (for a child); and (somehow) connected that with love and or affection. The problem is, our affection deficits are as deep as the Grand Canyon is wide.

Children only grow up so much. A man is a boy inside if he is a boy inside. A woman is just a girl inside if she is a girl inside.

"Grow the hell up!" we say.

Look around you. The world is replete with the fruit of our childhoods. We'd better get some serious brought-up-cy happening in this world or we'll be changing the diapers of 40-year-old men into 5030 (if we don't self-combust, collectively or individually, or if we are still here).

We cannot raise bad boys and hashtag away their sexual damned.

We cannot raise bad girls and hashtag away their sexual shit.

Our Sexual Heritage

Where were the judges and juries when Mr. Sexual Misconduct was being raped by his father? Where was society? Where were the judges and juries when children were sexing from age 3 or exposed to sex at age 4? Where are the judges and juries right now? There are still children in sex dungeons right now. We close our eyes to innocence living in sex hell and castrate grown men who are still children as if they are normal.

There are cultures where girls are taught by their adult women and mothers how to sex men; some of them at the age of 12. There are cultures where girls are taught by their mothers to use men for stuff ("civilized" cultures): i.e. gold dig. Whether we teach our girls to gold dig by gold-digging ourselves or teach them otherwise (verbally), they are learning. You cannot expect someone whose culture was sexual promiscuity and sexual deviance to be "normal" sexually. There is an unfillable gaping gap in the normal development of sexual tendencies for a healthy childhood versus an abusive one.

Many men and women are generations deep in sexual tendencies that are off-the-cuff for our present judges and juries, politicals and hashtags who call themselves normal. We have rehab for every other ill, but shoot sex power players and sexual criminals point blank. There is a severe and prevailing obsession to do that.

This is about more than extreme bad sex behavior. The fact that the poor bastards who have done the same are overlooked and select bastards with bank are publically castrated says this is a big money-power game or other forces are involved. Fair is fair. If indeed we can say we don't hate Mr. Power Player Sex Man and if we can say we don't have a beef with him, we have a basis for the current stream of addressing a thousand-year-old problem like this.

Tracing Us

Where did he or she learn that sex culture so different from ours? Is it different or bad? Oh the beauty of sexy sex! But bad sex is as vulgar as sex trafficking children and mangling their frail bodies with injury and inflicting their minds with horror. Most men and women with "bad" sex cultures come from environments and generations of bad sex cultures. For some, a certain "abnormal" sex culture is DNA. Bad sex culture is genetic. If you come to a normal sex culture with "Rules", you have to do the Rules or do the consequences of breaking sex laws.

The bad sex story is a veil of shame that covers our glory of being human greatness. The shame game places us at odds with destiny. We fight our own destinies that usher us into ultimate freedom.

Bad sex veils prohibit freedom. We don't see our destiny, nor our greatness, nor our God. We can only see us in our bad sex places that make us angry, trapped and victims. Instead of seeing who and what we are and what we are created to do, we hang our heads in shame and recoil. Rise up!

The world is spinning into chaos and we're lost in sex places and mediocrity. Your domain is over there, O King! That is part of why the world is sometimes so chaotic. The kings and queens – all of us – are tied up with mediocre things and sex fights instead of taking our places in the world. One man contributes so much to climate change and nations try to harness energy systems, while the other 7+ billion of us sit lost in sex, political, racial and social crises. Take your domain!

Irony

What is it about your life view that makes pedophilia your thing? What is your sex prude about? Why are you banging her and your wife is at home? Do you just like screwing someone's ass? Or, is there something else associated with it? Girlfriend, why are you sucking her? Why are you not sexing your husband? Why are you sexing your sister, your brother, your mother, your father?   Dig it up truthfully. We are all genetically inclined to something negative, not so good, or at least, something deplorable. You've got the image and likeness of God in you. Find that. Work that until your genetic flaws bleed out.

The power of darkness is obsessed with our pasts. That is the secret to its success in enslaving us. Emancipation happened but many slaves were challenged to find a new life away from slavery: some still are challenged to find life and live free. There are slave mentalities everywhere: black, white, rich and poor – sex slave mentalities, wealth slave mentalities, power slave mentalities, and so on. We tend to stay in slavery when we choose to defend what is most suitable to us instead of what is best for us. We love the feel good. Get the feel good and the good. The ego self will tend to what impresses flesh every day. You are bigger than that.

It is necessary to come out of the shame. How we come out is rooted in the heart of us. Unfortunately, many are emerging with a kill mentality for the bastards. In some cases, this may be the way to go, but it is a season of vulgar hatred that may be destroying us further or delaying us. It is possibly a season that could be counterproductive to superior destinies. Did we solve the problem?

CHAPTER 44
BUFF, THE BEAU

To experiment with sexing animals – bestiality or zoophilia – is to be curious, at least. That is what we call it - curiosity. Most of us will try many things for the first time to answer our curiosity. The experiment can go bad. It can go wrong. But, the experiment is at the mercy of the scientists. We are flawed and some of us have no god. The experiment happens again, ... then again. Soon, we see Buff lying on the couch or on his doggie bed like The Beau.

Some of our coy, taboo and blacklisting of sex topics comes from our behind-the-scenes "nasty". If you're sexing your dog, you don't necessarily want to talk about it nor bring that to the table of "normal" sex people. Keep it to yourself with your sex things if you want, but the stigma we place on sexy sex is as unhealthy as what some of us call sex and pleasure.

To the extent that we are sexing Buff (the dog), we have embarked on a different kind of sex journey than the intended sex journey. The problem with off-the-grid sex journeys is they are paths unknown to the human experience: paths that tend so far off the sex grid, we get lost in Forbidden. We now need Buff the Dog (BD) in our vagina or ass – separation anxiety can set in. This isn't as bad as the reasons why we find safety in such places.

The first time Buff's Beau got curious, he was bordering on I Can Be Psychotic or My Bent is skewed the Other Way. The second time, maybe the first did not provide sufficient information or he liked the first time. By the third time, check yourself. The lost places in us just tend to lost-further-in the-woods; many of these woods lead to depravity. This is a law just like gravity.

It is very powerful to discover that we may be lost. We have at least a thousand different paths we can take. Don't give up at such places; pursue the path that leads to a really sexy life. Talk that path through if talking helps you make sense of your places. Sometimes the places overwhelm and talking does not work. Don't give up on the really sexy life path and settle for one that leads to depravity.

WE HAVE NEEDS. WE HAVE EMOTIONAL, PHYSICAL AND SPIRITUAL NEEDS.

Having needs is normal. These needs are supposed to be met. When they are not met, we have unfillable and insatiable chasms of the soul to fill. We could spend a lifetime trying to fill them. Sometimes the journeys take us to impossible destinations to fill up. When we walk away from norms and engage our extreme curiosities, we are subject to whatever new norms.

If you sex a dog, a monkey or a beast, you create a one-bond with it. What does that mean?

Just having a bent to do a dog or animal tends towards other sex places than the places of a really sexy life. The original sexy intent of sex, our real sex nature, tends to a really sexy life.

What you think? Just the fleeting thought of sex with Buff is a seed. Watch your mind. Don't hold that thought. If you cultivate it, it grows. Just being in the presence of an animal with the mind to do should be sufficient to watch your mind. Come back. Our bent to sexing animals is about a level of depravity. Come back! We can go down the rabbit hole of the sex act, but at the place where we are considering sexing beasts, we need a jolt. If we are that desperate, it is too much desperation. It's not just about pleasure. It is a metric of your morality, like a thermometer to temperature. You indicator lights are blaring. Do what is necessary to dig up your bent.

It is a scary generational entertainment crisis with the constant cry, "I'm so bored". It is deplorable the extent to which we go for entertainment. Entertainment becomes a vice and the world weeps with our human imbalances. By the time we're dancing to the beat of having sex with our dog, we've digressed down the wrong path at the fork in the road. Sexing your dog is a step in the direction of inhumane human degeneracy that leads to points of no return, nor to glory. The problem is she will not stop at sexing a dog.

Sex File

In "Touch Me Lest I Die!", Bass was really just reaching out with palms stretched wide for something he craved because it was vital to his life. He just wanted to be touched. He was abandoned by his mother and never met his father. He was as cold and hardened as his world but he had never been touched to nurture, to connect. Sexing his dog was not about the sex at all. It was about being in a place where he had found a bond that was vital to his soul life. He never had that bond from his parents nor others. They did not nor could not nurture him.

Bass' Life World: Abandonment that led to severe emotional chasms.

Bass' Sex World: Acceptance from "unconditional love". Sex with his dog was about a place where he was accepted and had developed a deep emotional bond that was vital to his life. Unfortunately, he did not find that in his other relationships.

Bass is not the only person ever abandoned by his parents. Why Bass chose sex with his dog and others choose other sexual relations (some "normal") may be more than choice.

There are no untouchables, really. It depends on which side of belief we decide to cling. Bass is touchable but he must believe that and he must find Lover who can touch him like that. You have to decide which side of belief you will cling to – the side where you're untouchable or the side where there is someone who can touch you enough to heal you. You are worthy of touch like that.

Loneliness is a beast. If the train ever takes us there, we sit at the intersections. Honesty about being lonely can lead to better solutions than our "man-up" that says, "I do it my way!" And sometimes we have to just man-up or woman-up. If ever we find ourselves going deeper into depravity, we can turn around. Make sure it's not pride that keeps us going into depravity. No matter where we are, we are still touchable.

There is a beautiful sex place to discover. When we cannot face ourselves, sometimes we go for what we can face: some place that is less than ourselves.....

So we sing songs about having sex with our dog and our children sing along. Tomorrow, we will sing songs about having sex with robots, demons and aliens to pacify our souls. The dogs and demons will never be enough. Never. It's like prescription meds for the pain. Soon enough, 2000 mg is not enough because we've trained the pain to get louder. If we do not fix the pain, we need stronger dope or more 2000 mg. Nobody likes pain. When the dope no longer anesthetizes the pain, humanity digresses to where death feels much better. You're better than that.

CHAPTER 45
THE WILD SIDE

We take a walk on the wild side every time we sex our sex extremes without love. It's like playing with the devil; eventually, he takes you out. Sex and love go together like ying and yang, like bread and jam, like cookies and milk. Unlike other perfect complements, sex and love are more multidimensional, divine, kingdom.

Kingdom is such a ... It's a heavy word. Love has a kingdom. A kingdom has a king, authority, ways, laws and rules. If you respect the kingdom and play its game the way it should be played, it works for you. There is a price for violating the laws of the kingdom. We do not have to look very far to see this. Love has laws; love has ways. If we respect them, we enjoy the benefits of the kingdom.

Sex is a love kingdom phenomenon. Unfortunately, we keep taking sex out of its domain and trying to best fit it with our domains. The best of sex comes from its own kingdom, not ours. That is why some people are tying up a sex partner with chains and spiked apparatuses, whipping him like a wild beast to excite some kind of high and swinging from the ceiling beams (all at the same time). Go for it, Buddy, if it works for you. Be safe. May you come out alive and well: her too, or him. By the time you have to reconstruct your vagina from a few years of sex, know if that is sexing or abuse. There is a difference between "rough sex" and violence that comes from his shitty places. Get a lover.

That is just a good ass whooping with sex involved if you don't love him: if he does not love her. You've taken something that belongs to a domain and brought it into yours to play with it. The worst thing about our "sex" things is that we give sex this reputation that is not sex at all. That's our sex act rendition with penetration if the love is missing. That's your culture with penetration. Our sex corruption or rendition is sex games with penetration if the love is MIA. It may well be that you cannot have sex without love; not real sex. And that – what you're doing – is more of a sex act: not sex. That is your version of sex. True sex in all of its aspects of true is an expression that comes from love: not our version of love: from the kingdom of love.

So we reduce love to our lesser worlds to fit. It does not fit. It is necessary to get up to where love is to do love; that includes the sex. Then, some of us excuse ourselves on the "compliment", "Love is too hard": or the conclusion, "Love does not work": or the worldview of some of us that love does not exist. In our kingdoms, it cannot work because we are the king, not love. Love has its own kingdom that owns the sex. We don't own it, so we can only borrow aspects of it and adapt it to our ways. So we "break up" and have make up sex for drama or high. We need drama because love is too hard. The drama is excitement or something.

Power-tripping with sex is what we have always done, because we don't want to give up our power. We are our own god – normal. Extraordinary is human who can aspire to what we cannot accomplish with mere human means. Don't keep pulling sex into

your limited kingdom and expecting to get different results.
You've contaminated glory.

We will always have sexual harassment, sexual assault and bad sex hashtags with sex in play in our foreign kingdoms. Whereas love addresses the human person, the human soul and the human spirit to make sex one of the most beautiful and incomprehensible marvels we will ever have, our lesser kingdoms do not. We are all imperfect, flawed and human. Sex in the hands of the best of us without a higher power is a dynamic that will inevitably spiral into chaos. That is a fundamental problem with our world. We continue to take what is good and equitable and perfect and insist that it be a part of our imperfection. It does not work! It does not work! It does not work! It will not work! It will never work!

Sex outside of its kingdom of love will always produce some thing. It may even feel good. But, it will always fall short of its highest. That damn sexy thing you did last night that still has you on a sex hangover into late evening is not the best that it can be without true love.

CHAPTER 46
EGO

We find love to be corny (most of us). Once again, the love is not flawed. We have a lover most obsessed with one strand of hair that falls from our head and the ones that grow. Unlike us, this lover can handle such obsessions about each of us.

We have a lover who still awes at our nuances and marvels at our bent (good or bent to irreparable). He can take a lifetime delighting in how we sleep that way or what about yesterday made us cry so much. We have this excessive, extreme lover that is terribly blushy by the way we look at him. When we laugh well, he laughs hilariously with us. When we are puzzled, he feels it too, but has already figured it out before we even graced the stage of life. He waits until we are ready to figure it out. He is there while we bobble and stumble trying to figure it out. ....

This is only an infinitesimal fraction of this kind of love. Fall in love with that. Does she love you that way? Does your honey marvel at you like that? Don't waste your time on anything lesser. Of course, we are incapable of love on that level in our limited love capacities. Extraordinary ability requires superhuman. Extraordinaire love requires being imbued with extraordinary love ability.

This is a love worth being one with. Curl up to that every night.
You will never settle and love will be more valuable than trivial
sex acts.

Oh who has time for love like that? Who can do that?   Love like
that requires other. We have life so bank-heavy, to us a sexy love
like this is so ... utopic, impossible or Cupid-ish. If we spent as
much of ourselves on love as we do on bank, we could possibly be
successful at love. If we ever dare think like and be one with such
love, we'd be BANK; because this lover is bank. He is
superfluous in love, superfluous in health, superfluous in wealth,
success, life, ... Super lover is a voluptuous lover of an
otherworldly kind. The lover is a king. How's your lover?

We vest with our money. We make covenants and blood
covenants with our bank. But, when it comes to sex, most of us
trivialize it and cheapen it. Ode to the Kingdom of Sex! You
cannot reap voluptuous and invest trite. To reap voluptuous, you
must invest all. That is what the designer of the Kingdom of Sex
designed. All or nothing. Or we will continue to come up short.

Whether we understand it, know it or believe it, there is a part of us
that is spirit – immaterial, but real: aware, but mostly unknown (by
us): powerful, but unused/untapped; like God, but (mostly)
unaware of Him. Your strength is there. No-no. Not that – your
physical strength, your career ladder success, your intellect.
We've been endowed by the Creator with all of these and more,
but spirit-self is God-breathe. Our greatest strength is connected
to, is in, is because of, that which makes us most like God – spirit
self.

We sit in our glorious worlds holding onto our sex universe and
hierarchical systems and societies and factions like they are the

end-all and have no clue that within us is a God-breathe that has the ability to change the world (in an unprecedentedly good way). What does this have to do with sex and sexuality? You cannot change the image and likeness of God into din and expect for it to change this world into unprecedentedly good.

Our self-centeredness places us at the center. There's only so much you can do, Human. On our best day, with our greatest accomplishments, we will not aspire to a fraction of the potential of God. Self-centered rules our way. Self-centered lives our way. Self-centered sexes our way. It takes us away from sexing on a level that transcends this.

We are deceived enough to think that a nice kiss is love. It's a nice kiss. It's an infinitesimal step into a world we believe to be love. As big as that kiss may be, it is so small. If we could see the love that transcends this! If we could just get a glimpse of a fraction of that love, we'd give up our sex attempts for a moment with bliss like that.

You're bigger than trite love and sex blasé. The mightiest power player has not tapped his true potential if all she does is live from her greatness. All of our sex plays are just that folks. Inside of us is the image of one bigger than our pathetic heterosexual things, homosexuality, bestiality and Menage a Mille. He cares more that you are living that far beneath your human potential than the fact that you have sex with your mother. Sexing your sisters and her ten pitbulls is an indicator of our bent away from ... Superior. They will never be enough. Indicators indicate - location, planned direction, consumer price index (CPI), and so on. Our indicators place us here. Where do we want to go? Will we get there like this?

... Not if we continue on these same old failing paths.

CHAPTER 47
WE DON'T REALLY TEACH SEX ETIQUETTE

The power of ignorance is a breeding ground for sex que sera. At best, our children get lucky and forego the sex underworld. The powers-that-be behind the sex market, though? They can smell vulnerability like a pimp can smell filthy money. Oh, how dirty sex-slave pimps love innocence!

THEN: Children were exposed to whatever sex culture in their immediate vicinity.

NOW: Children can find sex online in a 4 or 5 gigabyte per second world all day and all night.

Feel-good just feels good, even to innocent children discovering or learning about their bodies. There are societies where sex and children are used in one sentence nonchalantly and cultures where Sex Ed happens in junior high or somewhere. We do not learn the art of human, nor the art of humanity. We bounce precariously from childhood to adolescence uninformed, misinformed, over-educated sexually, abused, or disgusted with him or her. We continue to miss the beautiful sex boat. We're still missing the beautiful sex boat into adulthood.

What is one cool thing about five-year-old Billy, Gina? What is one good thing about six-year-old Gina, Billy? Can you find another cool thing about her? Why is that cool? Why is Billy valuable to the human race? Why are you? Does Billy know? What is it about the pigtails, Billy? What in you is so attracted to them? Why doesn't Gina like you pulling her pigtails? Does she like it? What is Gina good at?

Five-year-old Billy and six-year-old Gina become 30-year-old Billy and 31-year-old Gina and still bobble to relate to the opposite sex on these levels: if they can relate at all.

We all have some sense of sex-related things – even before we know that we have a sense about sex-related things. The curiosity about the pigtails, the love notes to Jacob in second grade, the name-calling. How do we get our gender bent, our sex notions? How biased are they? How off? How skewed? How wrong or right? The beautiful God made beautiful sex beautiful.

How to get a beautiful picture of sex? How do we get a beautiful heart about sex? The beautiful God *gave* us beautiful sex. We have so many twists and agendas and biases on sex, "sex" stinks! But, the twists cannot bend sex out of shape. The agendas cannot control it. Our biases do not define it. They may bend us out of shape, control us or define us, but sex still is, ... beautiful.

Parents learned codes of silence so debilitating, their children eat the fruit of whatever they learned. They didn't talk about sex with their parents. Their parents didn't talk about the big "It". People did whatever was done and perpetuated whatever they learned. Retraining the brain to sex etiquette requires facing serious strongholds.

How do you shake that bad sex mentality to help your child? How do you shake sex taboos to help your daughter, Mommy? How do you crush the taboos to save your son, Daddy? Are you hiding that deeply that you'd prefer they die in sex plays that are killers. Give them "sex is beautiful" directives (appropriately) instead of the fears and the sex victimization.

One of the glorious ironies of our taboos is that they hide the good with the bad. Many of our taboos were created to hide the sex game so that the main players can keep the sex game in play for their benefit – to control is just one benefit. If the darkness has no tools nor arms to control the masses, it loses its power.

"Children are too young to talk to them about sex."

They are not too young to be victimized or learn the wrong sex plays. They are learning sex all kinds of ways elsewhere.

"Don't talk to strangers".

Perhaps, that is not a stranger molesting or sex directing your child.

The basis of our relational fiascos or greatness can be just as trained or directed as we train to be the best at our vocations and interests. We hardly teach successful humanity as intentionally as we teach CHEM 101. And for most of us, money is still the measure of success. Our relationships go for the money or the sex first, so who needs the rest of it? Then when women get emotional, we try to get him to engage emotionally instead of just being about us sexually. When he can't get her to do that in bed anymore, he checks out or finds a new Ms. Sex Ferocity.

Why isn't everyone that fascinating to us just because they are? Then sex comes from grand places of understanding the art of human. And the art of human comes naturally.

"Play the harps! The world is not like this!"

Change it.

CHAPTER 48
FRESHMEN 101

Our world is one of many broken, non-existent or unhealthy parental relationships; some of our parental relationships are WOW. Whatever they are, they have influence. Divorce affects the family unit in more ways than just split parents and money. It is vital, Daddy, to fill the daughter places that require something from you. There are lost son places too: sometimes even more than lost daughter places.

In a circle of college freshmen females (Ms. Freshmen 101), not a single one of them had a whole relationship with a beau, boyfriend or male their age. All of them came from divorced homes. In our circle of college freshmen, males (Mr. Freshmen 101) are still nervously coy about approaching freshmen females. They code and innuendo like Billy in the sandbox. Males disdain "Let's be friends". That is an insult. Communication and relating is as foreign as Jibbish but that is foundational to approaching someone you want to be more than just friends with. In our circle of college freshmen, all Mr. Freshmen 101 wanted was to try to sex their female college colleagues.

"So what? That is normal!"

Exactly!

We call this normal but why is our norm like this.

What trains most males and men to just be sexual? We are all trainable. The testosterone hormone argument is, but if your head game is in sync with "not just sex", men can relate better to women. On the other side of this college sex etiquette farce, females don't want to be the last one standing with "VIRGINITY" branded to their foreheads like a curse. Oh what a curse! College females want to be ... popular (more than understood). But, by twenty-something or 30-ish, she wants him to be into her *emotionally*; or be able to read her like that. All he can read (if he is lucky or paying attention) is her sex codes. By the time Ms. Freshmen 101 has advanced to the housewives of life stages, many of them are still acting like Gina with Billy in kindergarten. What is normal? Oh housewives can probably spank ass in bed, but relationally we are sandboxing.

With these human deficits in sex etiquette we expect for men to do something "normal" in the work place with relating to women. They've learned to USE sex. Women (many) have learned to manipulate the game. The proof of these relational deficits is all around – many men using sex and many women manipulating. And, then it goes vice versa – women use sex and men manipulate.

Nobody taught anybody what is normal sexual/gender behavior consistently enough for society to be infected with good sexual/gender/relational behavior. Nobody learned "normal" sexual/gender/relational behavior. You have to learn that. That means it must be taught and emulated and enforced. If daddy is missing, what does she learn about men? What does he learn? If relationships are broken who's teaching? The device?

We have to be real here. Get comprehensive about our sexual and gender crises or make another hashtag for 3020 2023 2025 and beyond. Mommy and Daddy, you are your child's first teacher. They learn from what you do. Mommy, they learn from you: even if it is you and the beau. What is your son learning? We cannot train our boys to be boys and expect for them to grow up and be men. We cannot train girls to do anything for a phone card or Phone X and only lock up the freak taking advantage of her "minor" underage status. She was prostituting herself to get $20 just like her mother taught her to use men for things. We cannot teach our children dirty sex games and expect for them to learn good sex etiquette. It just does not work. We have these sex contracts – spoken or just understood – and get appalled when they fail us.

The Groupie and The Star

Hey You!

Yes, you, standing in the line to screw the big Mr. Superstar. Does your mama know where you are or is she the one who trained you to screw men and try to take their souls?

Oh, she didn't train you to do that?

Who's your Mama?

Hey you, Super Star! Watch the groupies and the SEX WITH A MINOR thing. They will play that card. Watch the groupies and the star thing. They will also play the grotesquely fat harassment card but not before they slam the Hushbucks joker on the table. You're the Joker, Superstar, and they toast to the almighty Hashtag. Nevermind she's standing in the mile-and-a-half long line peeing up herself to screw your balls (and she's of age – old enough to be responsible for sexing a superstar).

Go home, Man. The dawgs don't like you. They will pay her to sue your superstar balls for harassment when it's time for the system to bring you down or when they need ratings. She will sue your superstar balls for harassment when she needs her next high (stilettos or dope). You're not all that to her, Superstar, because all you're worth is stilettos and dope to her. Inside you're God-man, but if you reduce yourself to her small pussy, there's a price for that – society price.

Level higher, Bro. The only thing to level down is your libido in the face of "infected" pussy. Nevermind the yummy pussy juice she swings and pumps in your face. She's writing a blank check for you to sign at the same time.

Back to Groupie: What the hell are you doing in his room? Go home.

CHAPTER 49
COMPREHENSIVELY SPEAKING: PARENTS

How does a 17-year-old teenage girl have a sexual relationship with a 35-year-old man? Where were her parents? At 17, why are you defying your parents and the law to be with a 35 year old man? Is the 35 year old man wrong? Hell yeah in this culture! By this culture's standards he is a criminal. But, Mr. Sex-With-a-Minor is not the only guilty person on this trip. Parents, you are responsible for your children.

We don't get to ignore our roles in the prevailing sex crisis as parents and command money from predators without considering our contribution to the crisis. Just because you got paid doesn't mean that you are free from your responsibility as a parent. A long jail sentence for Mr. Sex with a Minor (Mr. SM) does not mean your child is free and clear. "My child is free and clear" is the message we send to our 15-year-old Lenella Lea because we pressed charges with fury. What is wrong with Lenella Lea?

Many parents have accepted that their 16-year-old daughter is at the playboy mansion at 2 a.m. and their 2-year-old son just wants to overnight with a star. Many parents have accepted the deep generations of shame that is a part of their genetic code. In turn we've passed on deadly sex roots to our children. Defective sex codes in our DNAs are not reasons to condemn ourselves but to go to the roots and at least make an attempt to clean it up. If not for ourselves, for our children. Children are trainable and impressionable. Impress upon them what good.

Where is your daughter? Where's your son? Or are we just having children because having kids is in? What did you teach him? What did you teach her? We have a sudden sexual justice uprising that still does not address the shame game at the root. Some of the uprising is straight from hell and has a toll on humanity that is (in many cases) irreversible. The fact that we're not addressing all of the roots means we are really not about the sexual justice hashtag. If we really are, let's go to the roots: all of them.

The world has yet to find a serial rapist without a fault somewhere in his upbringing. Even when the stories of them boast a connected and well-respected family, there are killer roots and deficits lurking somewhere. What is the mentality of a rapist who believes in castrating women because his birth mother gave him up and didn't want him when he was all grown up? The roots of rejection are horrific blows to the soul that does not find a better path. These are killer roots. Ironically, rejection produces repulsion. The rejected repulses. Repulsion is contagious. It is powerful to know your story. What you do with the rejection and the pain changes the world – for better or worse.

The woe of victims and families of toxic root predators and decrepit relationships is a heartbreak that hemorrhages the heart of humanity to our current sex crises: and to the ghastly levels we cannot see. Without healing, our children will carry our bleeding hearts. One of the best contributions we can make to a sex crisis solution is to heal ourselves and be proactive about the bloody all around us. He may be the next serial rapist or killer. We are all a mother of nations. If 6-year-old Manly is emotionally wounded, what can you do to redirect his life to a good path? Our story may not be as severe as his and our story may not warp our belief system to the extent of serial rapist or killer, but one crooked line in our story can prevent us from our best life.

We all have at least one fault in our upbringing/our life. Most of us find our way forward anyway. To the victim of the criminal who tripped up on his roots, our nice statistics of "only one-out-of-one hundred million commit heinous crimes" is one too many. When society trivializes the victim because of the one rare case that went well, we dig poisonous swords into the wounded souls of victims. The value of one person is too much to take one victim lightly. Dig up the roots. Kill the bad roots. Plant some good ones. Sometimes the most effective bad root killer is an invasion of good roots.

When we accept destroyer vices – sex trafficking our children for any reason, making them terrorists for business or political deals, ignoring them to the mercy of sexual predators/predators - there are deadly root systems lurking beneath the surface. Ignorance? Maybe once, but again? Allowing our daughters to date him for status, fame, favors or money places parents in the game of prostituting their children. Insisting that our daughters date him for drama and ratings is the same. The public following on social media and TV that follows the matriarch who practices prostituting her daughters tells a vivid story of our unquenchable drama thirsts. The theme is the same – sex for something. Saying, "I didn't know" is now old. Especially when our children are minors. Why do you need the money, the sex, the fame, the dope so, Mommy? How can you get the bills paid legitimately? Do you have to do without temporarily?

"Do *without*!?"

Huh! We used to "do without": not these days. We do anything in order to live this we-want-it-we-gat-it-now life: to have like *them* (*them* is the proverbial joneses). We're supposed to all have more than enough. Unfortunately, the hierarchy of class is not built that way. On your way to having what you're supposed to have, work with what you have that you got by good means.

Killer roots aren't born in good places and out of good environments. They are nurtured and bred in something not good: in something sinister; something foul. Killer roots in the bloodlines of those who took from your great, great great great grandfather still affect you. You go after in pursuit – of the money, the dope, the game - because that thing in you is still trying to get back what they stole from you. What are we really after when we live our vices (at the expense of our children)? What drives us? It may be necessary to go back to our cultures and progenitors to see why we are okay with destroyers owning us and our children.

Cliché: "Leave the past behind".

Ideal, but the past is leaving us behind. Ideally, we can walk on to greater things without messing with the messiness of the past. The past is killing the human race, though. We either need to kill it or it will massacre the human race. And, since we seem unable to leave it behind, perhaps some of us need to deal with it. Perhaps the sex power-players playing the dirty sex cards right now will demand that we leave the past behind after they have slaughtered whom they please. And, of course, the public must comply because the "people in charge of the rest of us" get to tell us when it is convenient to regurgitate Mr. Bastard's past and not theirs.

Since we are too dishonest to go to the root, roots remain and prevail. Going to the root is not about shaming victims and predators. Going to the root is about fixing a problem. Since all players are not playing by the rules, we do not have consensus. There is a whole story. Who is saying the whole story? In the event that we are not saying the whole story, we are playing into the hands of the powers-that-be who hypocritically use the story for their power struggles. Checkmate, Poor Boy! Once again, you've been slighted. You lose. Again.

CHAPTER 50
MR. SM AND MS. SM

Caveat: There is a difference between the sexually active and the sexually abused. There is a story for minors who have sex. There is a story for minors who are abused, trafficked and molested. This part of the story (for the most part) is about minors who choose to be sexually active.

Today Mr. Sex with Minors burns for sex with a 15-year-old. Mr. Sex with Minors (Mr. SM) loves the innocence of youth. Mr. SM is another bastard we love to hang upside down by his balls over a flame like a pig crackling over a Hawaiian luau. Then we talk about it over coffee like last night's after parties. Let's not talk the agendas behind the agendas, here. Another more shining other side of Mr. SM is the story of the minors. They're shiny but nobody seems to see them. We love the riveting of burning Mr. SM's flesh more.

Minor – a person who is not old enough yet to have the rights that adults have.

They are the responsibility of an adult. A minor is the responsibility of an adult.

Minor – a person who is UNDER the age of full legal responsibility.

Sex is for adults.

Minors have parents. Parents are responsible for their minor children. Some parents are responsible for their minor children. Others know that their minor *thinks* she likes Mr. SM. If your 15-year-old daughter is attracted to Mr. SM, find out why. Parents know their sixteen/seventeen-year-old child. There are very few parents who do not know their fifteen-year-old daughter enough to know that she is capable of sex with a Mr. SM. It is obvious that all we care about is burning the bastard (Mr. SM or Ms. SM). If we cared that another child would be in the clutches of Mr. SM, we'd be addressing parents too, not just Mr. SM. We'd be addressing children – minors – whether they are twelve or seventeen. Parents cannot live a sex soiree and expect their children to behave sexually.

Mr. Smith, where is your 16-year-old daughter?

Ms. Jones, where is your 17-year-old?

Mrs. Dunmoree, where is your 7-year-old son? Why is he overnighting with an adult man?

Mrs. Dunmoree: Oh, he's overnighting with a very famous star! He's a famous man!

Mrs. Dunmoree, why is your 7-year-old CHILD overnighting with a man?

Ignorance is ignorance. By the time you're a parent, certain events are no longer innocent. By the time you're a teenager, you know more about sex lit than the "innocent" clause we like to use. You know if a penis is up your ass at 14, 15, 16, 17 or 18+: or younger. What are you doing at his place? Famous or not. Where is your mother? Where is your father?

If we continue to worship A-List as gods, it will be okay to sell out our children if that is what A-list wants. If we continue to worship our own vices over our children and ourselves, we will continue to sell out our children. We would swear that we do not worship our children nor ourselves. Worship is more than burning candles and hallelujah. If we care about our children and our grandchildren, instead of just hanging Mr. SM by his balls upside down over the flames, we would hold parents more accountable for their MINORS. After all, they are minors.

Unfortunately, children haven't learned the art of being children. Child means (at least) play well, obey your parents in what is good and learn; learn to obey what is love; learn to be in your world; learn to be responsible. We have these certain rites of passage in our cultures. By hell or high-water, we must lose our virginity by 16 lying among fields of grain or spread on the back seat of a car covered in steamy windows. We initiate children into drinking and give them a free pass to curfew-free and chaperon-free dating. And, children boss parents. Parents cow-tow to children like slaves and expect for children to respect them. They are children, teenagers and minors. Minors means they belong to parents who are supposed to be responsible for them.

If we really care about children the way we say we do, we would protect them better. So far, our lynch of bastard Mr. SM just looks like we have a really warped beef with Mr. SM (and we should). It looks like we don't give a shit about the next child that ends up with a Mr. SM. It looks as if we don't care much about the child or children who have already been with Mr. SM Bastard. It just looks like we are after Mr. SM's money, his balls and his life.

What about Mr. SM's wife or significands? For some Mr. SMs, his wife seems to have just found out all of these things or could not afford to lose her certain lux lifestyle while he was sexing minors. How dare anyone disrupt their lifestyle of bling to save a minor? How dare we question her?! Some of them really didn't know of their Mr. SM's extracurricular. This speaks volumes of our relationships.

What about Ms. SM? The new vogue of women and minors? Perhaps our beef with Mr. SM is so vehement because sex with minors is more of a sex thing with men: perhaps because there are less Mrs. SMs than Mr. SMs: perhaps it is because of our great "AHA!" when we can take down a man for something, anything. Mr. SM is so loathed, the Ms. SMs in our societies don't get too much press. The teacher with her young student is a passing blip on the screen of The Bad Sex story compared to Mr. SM.

There's a certain "intrigue" with the flick where the lady in hot pink feathers invites the teenage boy into her world for lessons (not piano). Teenager is fascinated to his boy core; not to mention the stories of his initiated peers in his head: stories of Ms. Feathers (Ms. SM) and them.   However society accepted these relations back them, they are still defined today as sex with minors. While they were some sort of cutesy thing with blushing teenage boy becoming a "man", did we ever find out what was really wrong with Ms. Feathers?

Today we're posting Ms. SM in her mug shot on social media with the headlines to shame her. Where are the students? Where did our sudden sex morals come from? Maybe, someone should have given the teachers who sex their students and Ms. SM a heads up that we had grown a conscience. Maybe the current sex police should have had a warning period for Ms. SM to bleed out her fetish for her underage students. Especially, since Ms. Hot Pink Feathers and her teenage boy was such "normal" entertainment before.

CHAPTER 51
WHY ARE MINORS SEXING?

The question is: Why are minors sexing?

What a stupid question! This statement is an indicator of where we are.

"How DARE we ask such a question!?"

If we really want to resolve the SM issue, we'd better ask the hard questions and answer them truthfully. For some reason, parents think that they have no authority with their children. For some reason, the roles have been switched with the child-parent relationship. For some reason, parents train their children (however implicitly or explicitly) to be sexually active. Some parents' sex lifestyles are so whacked, their children just follow. Parents live sex soiree or laissez-faire and expect for their children to do otherwise.

Sex has consequences. The C-word. "Consequences" got lost somewhere between Generation F and Generation AA. No matter what we choose to believe, there are still consequences. If you spend all of your money, you will have $0 (zero dollars). If you board a plane and fly from Denver to L.A., you will end up in L.A.

Maybe we just choose not to believe the consequences that we don't like. They still exist.

If a MINOR cannot deal with the consequences of sex, they should not be having sex. (Not even adults are supposed to be sexing if they cannot deal with the consequences.) It is critical to retrain our children about sex. Children shouldn't sex until they are mature enough to sex; by then, "children" no longer applies. There are adults who are not mature enough to sex.

Children are minors. Teenagers are minors. i.e. they should not be having sex. Why do we even have to deliberate on these subjects of minors sexing? They are MINORS. Let them find something else more productive to do that they love.

Nobody really really wants to be a forty-five year old virgin. So we try sex for the first time like trying a cigarette or a joint for the first time. Nevermind he is not at all attracted to you or is seeing you through drunken eyes. So what if you're just his side piece for the half-hour. He has a lot more pussies lined up for the next two hours and later.

Virginity isn't so much about age as it is about security. Girls and women lose their virginity everyday or give it away, so wander around breathless trying to find it. He took something from us when he "took" our virginity. He wanders around trying to slay his sex ways or demons with ass. Eventually ass is not enough. To him, you're a sex thing. To her, she lost something she cannot seem to recover.

Discussion versus Judging

The great silencer of the people is: "Oh you're judging me!"

We judge Mr. SM and hang him upside down by his balls over the flames but we're not allowed to *discuss* the fact that parents are responsible for their minor children. We're not allowed to say to

17-year-old groupie girl, "You know better than sexing a grown man." If we're going to "judge" Mr. Sex with Minors, who makes the rules to say we cannot "judge" groupie, her mother and her father? No one's judging. It's a vital discussion that can save our children or ourselves.

Why is Mommy allowing her 16-year-old a ticket to the playboy play pen at 2 a.m.?

Just asking – not judging. Where's her father?   If your Isha is that desperate to go out, Daddy, plan a date with her she cannot refuse; guide her to something that feeds her fancies. What feeds her fancies, Daddy? What are her fancies? Find at least one. Know it. Get it. (Legally.)

If we really care about children, we'd better start talking about them and the other sides of this burn-the-bastard Mr. SM or Ms. SM crisis. If Mr. SM rapes a minor, he is a heinous criminal of inordinate proportions. If Mr. SM has sex with a minor, he is a heinous criminal. If minor is sexing, it is out of context. Sex is for adults. If Minor is sexing and adults and parents allow it, it is time to deliberately and intentionally establish protocols for sexing minors. The contradiction is, we call them a minor but we turn a blind eye when they engage in adult activity. Perhaps, the law needs to be fairly written: A minor is only allowed to be considered an adult if he wants to be sexually active. Otherwise, we have fundamental social and moral contradictions that question our biased treatment of the SM issue.

Sex Ed

We educate children about homosexuality, transgender, acceptance, homophobia and all sorts of phobias, but refuse to educate children APPROPRIATELY about healthy sex and sexuality. Not Sex Ed the way we know it with our one term of sporadic, ineffective and sheepish classes in junior high.

We allow our children (minors) to have sex, but refuse to educate them adequately about sex.

A child is not an adult. A minor is not an adult. They should not be participating in adult activity. Or perhaps we should say: the drinking age is 18 but you can start sexing at 14.

In many cases, minors are sexing minors; and many parents know this. This may be why Ms. 17 thinks she's a woman and have a right to control her mother, or cracking voice 15-year-old teenager thinks he's the man and has no respect for his father.

It is undeniable that a child can learn, you CAN do this.

It is undeniable that a child can learn, you CANNOT do that.

Making it Better for Gen 2020 and Beyond

If we are sincere about changing the world for them, the best way forward is truth. The current Sex War wave may look promising, but it is predicated on contaminated foundations: foundations that only speak to predator. Sometimes it only speaks to predator if we have a beef with him or her.

Contaminated foundations crumble; look at history. One of the beautiful things about where we are is we have a proven model with which to see our world, our systems and ourselves. If nothing else, it is plain to see that we will return to such places if our foundations are unstable. Corruption, injustice and using people have always failed. May we find it in ourselves to build on truth. Somebody needs to build on truth. These are the only systems, cultures and norms that will produce true success. Our foes are otherworldly. Our means to win against them are inadequate.

CHAPTER 52
PREDATOR

The ways of a kingdom are in the heart of its king.

Predator is a different otherworldly kingdom. It is not from here
but it is prevalent here. It operates like our day-to-day. In the
heart of Predator is the ways of his kingdom. What is diabolical?
That is Predator's life blood. If you trace the diabolical, death and
evil, you will find the Kingdom of Predator.

Sex File

Authorities finally located the body of a missing college
student. It appears her Predator bludgeoned her and burned
her body before he buried her.

Months Later

Authorities find child porn on Predator's computer.

Watch the ways of Predator in this scene that played on the world
stage (only in part; there are more sides to the story). This predator
story is only one of countless. Many never make the world stage of
public opinion. Many are not so bodaciously stink. What really
happened here? Kink: pledge: attraction: sacrifice: other: or just

Predator? We don't talk about what else happened very much.
Predator is always there no matter what makes his prey vulnerable
or his kingdom happen.

Caveat: Everyone does not play into the hands of Predator. Some
of these events are just Predator. Some have another side to the
story that we keep in our secret codes, societies and places.

Our little bad dirty ways may not be on the levels of Predator's evil
but many of our little bad dirty themes rest in the foundation of
Predator's kingdom. Our shady little gray areas certainly are not
white. What are you contributing to? Who are you influenced by?
No matter how slightly it manifests itself, is it good? Without
justifying our little lies, secret cheats and sweaty intentions, is it
good? Or are we contributing to the influences of Predator's
Kingdom?

Heartless, merciless, deliberate vileness breeds and boils in the
heart of Predator. The blood of innocence – boys and girls – is
delicious perfume. For it craves innocence like forbidden delights.
It kills for such delights – innocent flesh. Child and goodness
makes the kill more tantalizing. It kills for fraudulent dainties –
the price of 5-year-old prostitutes, the screams of victims, the
adrenaline of winning. There is no pleasure in honest and good.
Oh, such humane attributes are deadly poison to its damned
agenda. It inflicts patriarchs and infests matriarchs with its
venomous play and roars silently, vehemently on the stages of
human affairs. Families: lovers: societies: politics: kingdoms: and
nations: these are on Predator's hit lists.

So a man would give his soul for the lure – freedom, power,
wealth, women, money. In Predator Kingdom: Freedom is
licentious; Power is control; Wealth is fraud; Woman is lust that
kills; Man is bitch; Money is a bargaining chip to get the kill. The
kingdom of Predator loves the souls of men. Each child a

perpetrator abuses makes Predator's kingdom stronger and contributes to his momentum of hell. This is the story of Mr. 50 Wives.

The problem with Mr. 50 Wives or Mr. 28 Wives is he has no limits. He eats sex for life like we breathe air. So a child is succulent childsplay. Polygamy was the forte of ancient cultures from Africa to China. For certain Daoist, it was a sign of wealth and power. In some of these cultures, the habit of many wives spilled over into other sexual extremes, including sexing virgins and children. Our modern Mr. Polygamist has no limits, really; because any of his demons directs the sex plays in his collection.

By the time he pinned his son (a child) to a floor (a covenant) to get off with his devious child porn acts, Predator lived possessed with the demons of his progenitors, cultures and societies. By the time he taught his son to rock his sweaty ass, he carried the predators of his progenitors in his soul. Predator's father perpetrated child porn acts on him. Predator's grandfather ate devious lust – his twenty wives, his helpless two-year-old daughters, his fifteen-year-old daughter wife.

There are no lines: no distinctions with lust in the hands of demons. Demons because by the time devious lust is your master, you've left the realm of human realties. Demon lust lives in its own world. This size lust leaves no room for you to bargain with it; it owns.

Predator travels like ghosts and creeps like fire. The world is at its feet. In Thailand, its sells the world's children for guns and money. In Africa, it rapes women and children with bloody machetes and damned automatic rifles in hand. In America, men sex and molest boys in closets. In the "church" (some of them) they sex and molest whomever they choose. In political halls, they uncover his sidepiece for his horrified wife to discover, his media to gloat and his rivals to try to succeed him. His rivals have made deals behind the scenes of politics with money games the public never sees. In the halls of fame, they take down a sex power player to accomplish their agenda.

The hidden societies love Predator. They are just as guilty as the father indulging in sexual licentious acts on his child. Father Priest on Altar Boy wreaks of a predator-prey mentality rooted in power and control games. Some of the "prey" in these sex relations - Father Priest/Altar Boy, Father/Son, Adult/Minor, Society Power Player Dominant/Submissive - normalize their experiences; some adapt outlier sex lifestyles: some choose heterosexual lifestyles: some choose homosexual, bisexual or polysexual lifestyles. Even where the prey can normalize the world of foul sex plays, they contribute to the intent of Predator where demons slither and perpetrate.

"Oh, I don't do little boys."

Of course not. There is a kingdom that does little boys. You just happened to survive that part of that kingdom. They're still doing little boys. Little boys are dying there. Little boys are becoming men with devastated little boys inside. Some are barely surviving; others are bringing their shit to the world and marrying someone's child; others are killing themselves because of their atrocities. Sure, you're okay. What about them? What about your son? What about your daughter? What about theirs?

CHAPTER 53
PREY

Today, the son of a King Predator killed himself. It was the only way he knew to silence his demons. The demons are the killers in the minds of victims: in their souls: some demons take over the body; the demons are otherworldly. He battled every day in his mind with a world of sex so demonized, he took his life. The world marches on. It always does.

We have yet to say who draws the lines between normal and abnormal sex games. We like to say such games are people's personal business. While one waves his Bible, another waves his pleasure principles; another yells the tenets of his religions and his gods; another vows in blood to his society.

Unfortunately, there is a victim in our belief systems that defraud another human being. We prosecute the white collar embezzler and send troops to slay the rebels taking territory in jungles and deserts that have to do with our money, our wealth. They threaten our wealth, you see. And if the sexually victimized happen to be in our oil zones, war zones and wealth zones, we could possibly use their plight to come and wage war. And not until the demons who taunt sex victims touch our bank do we pay attention. It must be enough that the soul of victims die in sex slavery that is devious enough to kill – by suicide or other.

There is no way for a 3-year-old, a 14-year-old, a 26-year-old, nor a 50-year-old to carry the vexation of years of dirty sex games that suck life like a python. In a good scenario, the prey finds a way to live a good life. In a world where the demons of the past torment the heart, the soul and the life, a victim lives in the slums of bad sex torture. Until the value of one human being is more valuable than our trite sex plays, there will ever be prey. This 26-year-old prey died today.

Today he said, "Goodbye"
To a world that could not save him
His guilt, his shame, his pain
Too much to bear

He died a long time ago
At four or five
As usual his early days of molest in dark places
Were too young to remember filthy details he fought to forget
He could not forget the pain
The torment
Vile torment
Took his life away

His father his keeper
Was his father his fiend
Was his father his haunt
His predator
His pain

"Thank you, Father", he says
"Thank you for the pain
For the fears
For the insecurities
In them I see a reflection of you
Your dirty face

Staring me down like meat
Your demon-dripping hands
Touching me
Your breath a stench of anger
Of your years gone by
What have they done to you?
You hurt so much"

"I cannot carry you, Father
Grandfather
And their years
Your souls I cannot bear
So Goodbye
One last time
Goodbye"

To the children who still live in the closets. To the children who
never make it out. To the men who walk free in chains. They live
in manly places with a terrified 5-year-old boy inside. To the
women in stilettos carrying her 3-year-old self. They live in
women's worlds with 4-year-old bleeding heart.

CHAPTER 54
WHERE WAS HIS MOTHER?

Every mother is not ready to be a mother. Sometimes life comes at us so fast, we are still struggling with our own pain. We are fighting a drug thing, an emotional thing, a past thing, a boyfriend attracted to our insecurities: and so many other things we fight, struggle with or live with.

Ideally, we come to motherhood with all of our "ducks in a row" emotionally, personally, financially and physically. Ideally, we have a fairytale man who is a dream with kids and by our side. Unfortunately, that is rarer to most mothers than a pink diamond rock on their wedding ring finger. We should have all of the parameters right and our ducks in a row so that we can run through flowery fields with our children giggling and free with a skip half-step all day, every day; and sweet, happy dreams at night. Life hardly happens that way.

Mommies work: some two and three jobs (sometimes daddy is the only parent). Daddies are absent a lot of the times; some of the times Daddy is a Predator; sometimes Boyfriend is: sometimes relatives: often, a stranger. We don't have to go back very far to find the latest 3-year-old child allegedly killed by Mommy's boyfriend. Everyone is not trained to supervise children; some children are left in the hands of adults with problems; some are left with children.

It's hardly a blame game. It is necessary to solve problems. When children continue to be fatalities, it is necessary for society to step in: either to secure them or provide safe haven for them while Mommy is at work or "legitimately" unavailable. One children's hospital has seen a 29% increase in child abuse *fatalities* from 2017 to 2018; they recorded a 200% increase in child abuse-related deaths from 2016. This is a horror. If we continue nonchalantly with child-victimization, we have the blood of innocence on our hands. That is too much to bear. Fix the problem. If we hope to change the game, we must look at all of the sides.

The Children

Comprehensively speaking, we must ask questions of our mothers. We must ask of our fathers too, but a mother is still (for the most part) the first line of defense for children. If the father is the only parent, he is responsible for his child(ren). We are still the product of a mother and a father. If one is sick, demon or foe, we can hope that the other is well enough to save her child: his child. We must ask questions of a society that fails children. We must provide safe places to assist mothers in order to save our children. Of course that is not our responsibility. The responsibility of a child rests with his or her parents. Unfortunately, we have societal ills that affect children. This brings home problems to our society. We are granted the opportunity to influence a child in a positive way while Mommy or Daddy is away or add another 3-year-old girl or boy to the fatality count. What were they born for?

We must ask questions of a society that molest, abuse and kill innocent children. We must ask questions of a nation that allows the cycle of outlier societies to breed their ills on the innocent and prey on the prey. If there are laws about sex with minors, why does a man have teenage wives? How does a teenage mother protect a child? How does a child not become a young man and sex his father's wives? Where does he get his sex norms?

When a man loses his sense of normal, when does society step in? Why did society allow a Predator who molested his son free reign so long with so many wives, so many children, so much poisonous freedom? Unfortunately, for his son, a victim of suicide, it is too late.

Walk away, women. Take your children when it is safe and run to freedom in safe places. Society, provide safe places for women and their children from abusers. Mom, the price you are willing to pay to stay in places with a man owning twenty or two wives, or in a place with a man abusing you is no place for children. At the very least, it is confusion for a child: confusion that takes a gun to his brain and blows it out of his head to silence the demons that he met in filthy places where his father brutalized him with sex games from his father's own demon soul. You cannot play sex games with a man of sex demons and be free. His demons have a way of getting inside you.

And so it goes... Competition between women breeds well in environments of fighting to be the pick of the night. Even when we ban together for faux solidarity on an issue where hatred for HIM fuels our war, it is still hatred. Underneath, the DNA of insecurity runs through the code of women subject to being One of the Wives and His Sidepieces.

The seething of brewed hatred, animosity and jealousy amongst women from the beginning is erupting and still burning hot lava underneath. Welcome to causes, hashtags, sex politics and take the bastards down. Panty and bra burning has taken on a new face – Take the Bastard Down.

The upside? We are learning who we are; some of us know who we are – vital, resilient, image of God. Live from that. The bitterness is poison.

CHAPTER 55
SHAME GAMES

Eighteen-month-old Jane in the pink frilly dress kissing Billy
sitting next to her in the powder blue jumpsuit goes viral. Pulling
pigtails in the sandbox is still cute. So where does the innocence
go? With knowledge comes responsibility. With our limited
knowledge about sex and sexuality comes shame. The shame is so
prevalent, most of us are genetically coded to blush at anything
sex. We are genetically coded to hide anything sex. Something
tells us what we are doing is wrong. In places where we have fear,
there is a great proclivity to control. In the hands of Power-
Trippers, control is a beautiful, deadly weapon.

Who told Billy that he should be ashamed to like a girl or kiss her?
When did he lose his innocence? What are our social memes, our
cultural inbreed, our familial ingrain, our biases that make
anything about the opposite sex coy at a certain age?

We must address the sex from the roots to win the shame game
that leaves us vulnerable, passive, fearful and targets of
manipulation. Jane (the cutey kissing the hottie) is still growing up
with sex tendencies that sit her with a boss who makes a pass at her
and she thinks that she has to stay. Jane is not the only one. Until

we address the sex root of us, the sextalk is just trendy nice. If we want solutions, we have to go there. Today, where we sit writing this and reading this, sexual improprieties are in play in silence.

If we get real, really real, we can destroy demons instead of swatting at gnats.

Demons: those otherworldly forces you keep succumbing to as if you have no power within yourself to defeat them; even when you find the roots of them.

Shame makes us hide. It makes us cover up. Sexual shame closets mute us from talking the real roots of our sex ways. Today, sex shame is happening. The implicit ways of us that cause direct sex shame is even more prevalent – hiding your 5-year-old's eyes when prime time kisses and rolls around the sheets: blocking that on their device.

Don't block?

You better block.

There is a lot to block, but there are places to talk about what and why you're hiding that. Curiosity defies blocks.

They didn't talk about it. Our parents didn't talk about theirs and their parents didn't talk about theirs. We can go back as far as a human race and find sex plays in violation of good and sex plays people did not talk about. The taboo is a control freak, at least: a killer at its most extreme. So, we sit in a world of civilized people paralyzed with debilitating shame from every gamut and culture of sex, when the maker made sexy sex sexy and good. Cultures and individualism aside, we find a sex maker who said, "Let your lover send you reeling and her breast satisfy you".

We can't talk about "bad" sex, so it stays in the subconscious or conscious, suppressed voluntarily or involuntarily. Ultimately it affects: sometimes everything. It affects our communication. There's almost a film, a tinge, a haze, a cloud (of shame) when our sex experiences are bad. We get trapped behind the shame fog and live from there. Or we fight to come out. The current fight is so ghastly, it's worse than sex shame that makes sexy men impotent and wonderfully Divalicious women putrid.

Shame prevents us from success and from living our full potential because we are afraid. Only fearless = free. We were not created to be intimidated by sex, sexual improprieties, nor our skewed sex ways. We were created to be free: to live and enjoy living in the context of good. The fact that we are intimidated means that we have fear. However infinitesimal, however gross, it is fear. The power of shame holds a human race at limited capacity of greatness, because we are afraid to go to the root of the sex game. If we do not dig up the root of the sex problem, we will have more sex problems. Tomorrow, twenty years from now, our children will live another sex problem in their generation that is worse than ours if we don't kill the roots.

CHAPTER 56
THE CODE

"You can be at least a thousand times more than what you are."

We live in our small spaces, with our limited capacity using only a fraction of our potential and functioning at a fraction of the ability that we possess. There is within each of us a code more than our human DNA and our experiences.

The sex, dope or other high we had last night or last year does not even compare to the God code within each of us. Our 2-minute or 60-minute sex highs, whips, balls-and-chains, muzzles, chandeliers and Doberman ecstasy is an infinitesimal speck of who we really are. Is that all you've got? A 10-minute high?

Imagine if we could possibly tap a fraction of our real potential. Don't walk out of here limited to that – whatever your sex file, whatever your life file. Find the code that makes you god. What's your domain? What is your kingdom?

How arrogant!

Do you even know that you have a kingdom?

There is within you a kingdom most infallible, generally untapped:

unlimited. That is the code. If you're not living that, you still have so much more to tap.

Your bent is where you have a tendency to go. Our bent is not as important as why we are bent that way. We have been cultured to let be by now. What we decide to "be" shows a "fault in our code" or flawless genius.

The Root

We all have something that wows us to stupendous wonder. We stand speechless in awe of it and forget our human existence if only for a moment – that view from the heights of the Himalayas, the first Aurora Borealis of the season, the face of humanity on a sidewalk or in a favela. That place of stupendous wonder is just an inkling of a world so grand, we are ill-equipped to live in it. That is the world of flawless genius. That is the view of grandeur so insane it fakes us out to think Utopia is real. Ah! But that is the world with roots so damn sexy, it will tap dormant potential that can change the world. That's the world of damn, beautiful sex.

That world has its own principles, its own culture, its own power. It has its own roots. They're quite golden, but they are the driving force of that world.

On the other hand, the other worlds where we live have their own too. They have their own views, systems, laws and principles. They have their own roots and the force that drives them drive them to maintain the purpose of their world. Purpose: what it is here for?

No sensible person can look at an addict afflicted with cocaine blood and consider it good. The addiction isn't what or who the addict is. It indicates something about the addict's life world. A church fanatic is because of their life world... sometimes. A racist is heavily influenced by whatever their world was or is.

Our bent away from the world of ruthless perfection takes us so far away from the sexiness of such a stupendous world. "Sexiness" meaning the raw perfection of that world. Do you know who you are? Not your parents, genetics or accomplishments. You are endowed with a code to live ruthless perfection. Not perfect. Boom good.

Our life's journey is a treasure of knowledge about our personal culture: our ingrained beliefs. Our life's journey is a treasure of knowledge about our personal sex world. The Life is: the way we lived: the journey that brought us to this current place.

You are sexing like that because your life is/was like that. Your God-image got messed up in the Journey of Life. Your Journey of Life presented you with some very stink places that made you respond like that. Or, your code from *their* (your progenitors') Journey of Life got rewritten to include parts of their code. Now you are so far away from the original blueprint.

Their Journey of Life: all of the life, experiences and environments of our archaic family tree.

Sometimes it is a part of the Journey of Life to get hurt, wounded and even obliterated. How we respond is individual to us. We can offer hope instead of despair all we want, if she chooses despair, then that is what molds her life. It is horrifying what some of us face in the Journey of Life. It is brutal and vicious. Sometimes we choose other than the convention. Sometimes hope is nowhere on our list of choices. Sometimes we create our own normal to survive the excruciating, inhumane despicables. Somehow we manage to arrive ... somewhere. It is vital to ask, "Is there somewhere better?"

Is there some place better than your normal? No matter how grand your normal is, have you arrived? Not arrived to the height of your best. Have you arrived to some place so grand, your best cannot take you there? Are you cheating yourself of *that* Grand? Your life - not your money, your status, your network – could be robbing you of your most royal self. Is your life opulent success or just *your* Grand?

Your life is so far beneath opulent success if you are a product of choices from despairing shit places. Opulent success is not an illusion. Oh, the frailty that traps us in Limited! – Limited mindsets: limited relationships: limited love: limited status: limited bank: limited life: limited sex. The root of the kingdom that makes us live limited keeps us from extreme potential that we are capable of. It is a kingdom most opposed to the love and beauty of opulent success.

CHAPTER 57
LGBTQ

It is one thing to *desire* acceptance.
You are accepted.
You are loved.
It is another to *demand* that the world accept your sexual
preference(s).

Most of the world doesn't give a shit about who's who anymore
compared to their personal crises. There are still people trying to
find a decomposed, maggot-laden cockroach in the garbage to feed
their five bloated-stomach children. In other words, our world is
one of perspectives. And sometimes, for the most part, just live
your life. For those of us who may be trying to understand
homosexual or LGBTQ [LGBT2Q+, LGBTTQQIAAP or as
preferred], we must be fair and open-minded if we are really trying
to understand. For the homosexual and LGBTQ community who
want to be understood, it is necessary to be fair and open-minded.
Like any other lifestyle or cause, forcing our preferences on others
is as counterproductive as ebb and flow.

We've used "homophobia" in a very broad way. Many people are
really just trying to understand. Every non-gay person who
disagrees with gay is not "homophobic"; just like every white

person who voted for a white president instead of a black one is not racist. People get to choose what they believe and what they do. If in our believing and doing we preserve the good of humanity or make humanity more like God-mage, we are all more successful. To the point that our believing and doing robs ourselves and the human race of God-image, we are unsuccessful. Try a different approach.

If you are white and nice, you are just a nice person who is white (race). If you're white and messed up, you are just a messed up white person. If you are gay and nice, you are just a nice person who is gay. If you're gay and messed up, you are just a messed up person who is gay.

The LGBTQ dialogue is an attempt to understand for those who sincerely want to understand. The dialogue is not to have negative attitudes towards anyone in the LGBTQ community. If you are LGBTQ, be deliberate about educating others who are open and let it go with the those who disagree and with the haters. Just because they disagree with you does not mean they hate you, are afraid of you or are prejudice against you. Some people just disagree with you. People who are haters are an entirely different class. Haters are haters. They hate themselves and Jesus. Don't expect for them to like you and don't take them so personally. They have a history too: so does church people, the religioso, faith-based, the culturally-biased, Mr. White Collar criminal and pedophile. At what point, does the LGBTQ community turn the table on themselves and start hating back? At that point, LGBTQ becomes just like the haters. It's all hate.

Christian, gay, Muslim or trans, we don't get to force our beliefs and ideals on people. Being bigots certainly does not invite him or her to our lifestyle. If Sam don't like you, so what? Sometimes the LGBTQ stance to the homophobic and haters places gay in a dark light. Don't mistake an attempt to understand you or someone's belief system for homophobia. Gay haters are as Christian haters are as women haters. It's still hate.

Sex File

Today, authorities found her body, burned beyond recognition, in a car. The murdered transgender woman was a loyal friend, a passionate dreamer and a heart who loved people.

She had big dreams like most of us and she loved just about everyone. She wanted to live those dreams like the rest of us, but she didn't make it. If it is not too insulting and just for here, we call her Dream Lover. Dream Lover was not the first transgender murder case this year. Officials count eighteen (that they know about). Last year, the count was 26. Where does it end?

Was her killer afraid or threatened by her choice? Perhaps. Her killer is a killer. The homophobic must look at the Whys of their fears and address them. Fundamentally, where we lose our respect for any one person we stand at the threshold of crossing the lines. It is vital to figure it out. We can best do that with honest communications – more with ourselves than the rest of the world. If we can own that thing inside our self that hates him or her, the world changes because we are the master of our self. There is nothing that they can say to you to change you. You have to do that. Education about LGBTQ is powerful. Only we can do what it takes to change ourselves.

If we – all of us – really knew who we are, we wouldn't settle for places that keep us labeled. Take flight to better mindsets, cultures and love protocols that make the world worthy of its name.

Choices

Why why why do we need the rest of the world to accept us and our sexual preference so? Perhaps it is because we do not believe in ourselves nor our choices. Why does he, she or that have to validate us and our sexual preferences? The lengths to which we go to exact respect or acceptance or validation from the rest of the world speaks volumes of our faith in ourselves.

Why don't you believe in yourself enough? Dig that up. Before we spend ourselves to do that, we would fight, claw and kill the masses to accept us and our sexual preferences: we fight for them to believe in us: give us their stamp of approval. Do you approve of yourself? Then live! If you don't, you need to find out why you do not believe in you, your choices and/or your sexual preference. If we come from a truth that has discovered why we choose that lifestyle, we have a better story to present to those from whom we demand respect. Everyone else must earn respect. Why is it okay for you to demand acceptance and the world comply?

A slave to anything steals our God-image. A slave to anything and anyone robs you from your true inheritance, your true identity. Don't let the crises of a defective and abusive childhood rob you of your best life because you are pissed at them: or everyone. Our leaders are supposed to facilitate that. The best life is possible for every person; it is in us to live that. The greatest leaders have the ability to bring that out of every person. Leaders aren't limited to government titles as much as "leaders" are those among us with influence: like media, prevailing organizations, personalities and status. That is one of the reasons why we continue to fail. Our markets, our systems, our economies, our nations fail, because we are so far removed from who we really are.

Most of us were presented with the option to be gay, straight, heterosexual or extreme. What did we choose? Why did we choose that way? If we are honest and fair, we could find our truth and live more successful lives. Until we are really truthful, we have no basis to refute truth nor come to the table. That is a waste of time. The melodrama of talk is a futility without honest truth that confronts every aspect of us. Take a number with the rest of the melodramatic people feeding the status quo – high social media likes gone viral (HSML). Nothing wrong with HSML. When you come away from the last post, what do you have? Don't live from a proclivity to anything when you can have a damn prosperous life.

A damn prosperous life: A life that makes you live from something more powerful – like ridiculously opulent success.

CHAPTER 58
THE SUBMISSIVE AND THE DOMINANT

A man is never a Submissive to or less than another man. NEVER! Rich or poor, king or peasant, slave or free, a man is never less than another man. One of the codes of The Submissive and The Dominant in ancient sex cultures was that the man being penetrated sexually was The Submissive and the penetrator was The Dominant.

(All things being equal – i.e., given "normal" sex practices: What does this say of a woman? Is Woman always supposed to be The Submissive? Does this Dominant-Submissive code carry over into the mindset of woman being lesser and being treated that way? Just asking...)

There are societies of men that still penetrate another for this reason. He penetrates his submissive to train him (like a dog) to be submissive. You are a man. You are not less than any other man. Do not give your man away to anyone nor anything. Anything that demands of you what makes you man in exchange for slave is abusive. We live with societies of men abusing men to elevate themselves. Then they have the audacity to call it "brotherhood". Brotherhood does its little charity coverups to legitimize reducing a man to less than God-image then Submit-and-Dominate behind closed doors to rank men. That is deplorable! Man, if you allow that, GET UP! You are a king!

Brotherhood, in the higher energy of spiritual dynamics, you condone, allow and perpetuate that thieving spirit that any man is less than another. You attempt to defy man's creator that made him to be as his God. Why are brotherhoods, societies and orders sexing boys and minors? No, no; not morally why are they doing it? We know that morally it is wrong according to our laws. Get behind the scenes of what is really happening. Why are brotherhoods, religious orders, societies and the big boys clubs sexing men and boys? Why does a man want to own another man? Why do grown men train boys to be slave? We're wasting our time with The Sex Crises if we fail to get behind the scenes of our sex things. This kind of ingrained domination trains men, boys and societal ranks so indelibly, The Submissive would do anything for The Dominant.

Homosexuality is bigger than sex; so is sexuality.

Sex is bigger than sex. The feel good or feel bad of sex is only a fraction of the ramifications of sex. We get hung up on the physical part so much, we fail to realize the incomprehensible, multifaceted worlds that sex and sexuality are. And, if we can place sex and sexuality in light of who we are, they are placed. They are not owners; we are.

We are bigger than all of that. We are bigger than the money, the dick, the sex, the power playing, the societies' mantras. We have a higher nature! We have a higher nature! WE HAVE A HIGHER NATURE! Operate from that! GET UP TO YOUR HIGHER NATURE!

Do we think about the fact that a boy molested or submitted in our societies and orders becomes a man? The boy learns his sexual bent from there. He is cheated of his freedom of mind to choose based on what he wants. Instead, he has a propensity to what he was taught. We are prone to boasting about the one percent (2% or whatever relatively insignificant percent) of molested and abused from these societies and organizations who find a wonderful sex life. If the only thing a community of sex outliers perpetrated on the innocent was sex, we would "only" have victims exposed to sex "Other". It is never just about a little high for Priest, Saint, Baal or Demon. It is always about something more sinister (whether we realize it or not). The 26-year-old suicide victim is one of many who fight the sex demons every day. And if we think for one second that it is only about a Father getting off on a boy, we are most ignorant in the ways of the kingdom of darkness. Here, Here, Here!

When we become privy to the ways of the kingdom of darkness, we are qualified to determine the extent of our sex swag.

When we are honest to the fact that innocence is impressionable to what he or she is taught, we have a basis to bring all of the sex cards to the table for the best of humanity. Until then, we are ill-equipped to say that what we did to an altar boy or a child has no bearing.

Check your bent. Why are you bent that way? Why is she bent that way? Once again, nobody wants to hear The Perpetrator Story. We want to stop the sex crisis but we don't care that Perpetrator was an altar boy. We don't care that Father Priest was an altar boy too. (Not excusing: just bringing some more of the cards to the table.) We don't care that Sexual Harassment learned that from the places he's been. These are the places we refuse to address and dig up. We cannot have whole societies if we continue to ignore Perpetrator.

Perpetrator needs to be addressed comprehensively; not just legally. Perpetrator needs rehab. Some of them need what society cannot give. If we love the drama of The Bad Sex Story as much as we do, it will continue. And if we really love The Bad Sex Story that much, we need Perpetrator. And if it is a love of The Bad Sex Story thing and a drama thing, we need to leave Perpetrator alone. It is unfair to feed our drama from Perpetrator's shitty past. This sounds really ass to most of us. And we will respond with incredulous, "OMG!" (and perverse profanities) to the presentation that we love The Bad Sex Story. If you hate it, kill it. If you want to kill it, you have to heal Perpetrator or get rid of him or her.

Demons don't just die.

CHAPTER 59
PREHISTORIC SEX: SHORT LIST

Generations, traditions, cultures and societies still mess up the sex with our ways. Our modern day societies, cults, orders and religiosity are just a contemporary spin on what was: it just looks different. Societies, organizations and cult-ures still make laws, covenants, oaths and rules. Organizations, orders, cults and religiosity still have hierarchies of systems. May you be a top gun.

From the Ancients to the present century, kingdoms, empires and nations have come and gone. Sex and sexuality were always players. Sex and sexuality are players. Sex and sexuality will be players. However directly or indirectly, sex and abuse played a role in how life was in most societies.

Our modern "records" of prehistoric sex are right in line with biblical records - anything from multiple partners, orgies, incest to bestiality were on the sex agendas. Females took advantage of their multiple orgasms prowess and males waited their turn for a go at sex with females. Free-for-alls only became less free when the question of inheritance came to the table; (today, some of us have enough conscience to think about STDs.) Back then, males had to consider who their property would go to with children here, there, tither and yon; so once again, one power-player met another. i.e. Sex met Money.

The thought of Mr. Prowess' money going to the son of Ms. Popular was not so attractive for many of the men in the Mr. Prowess clans; this was enough to curb Mr. Prowess' appetite and for him to consider the real consequences of his sex free-for-all. (So we *can* control ourselves; we just need a good enough incentive.) Nevermind. Today they have law, agreements and contracts for our free-for-alls (although these are often contested).

So, women learned that they were as important as his money. No wonder women still go for the "bastard's" money these days – she knows that is what is most important to him: more important than her. There will always be at least one woman who will game you, Mr. Prowess. Oh, and the audacity to tell her someone else is better than she is titillating. Let the games begin, Prow Prow! It's on when some of us believe we have a rival that he thinks is better than us. Ah, and so we've bred women and men like this in our societies. So, Hello Now! They're out for the kill! (Not to mention, this one is a pre-election year.)

Sex File

One of our famous divas had a short-term relationship with one of her temps. Her greatest joy and crowning achievement from that one? $20K in Hair and Beauty from *that* one.

Who knows what she got from the other ones? Who knows how long she played this game before she met this one? Who taught her and how much did she get from the others? In certain Gold-Digging Circles, $40K is a fraction of a speck of worthless dust. Whether our gold-digging schemes are to make a living or for vengeance, the ancient cultures live on in our current arenas of sex wars, crises, hashtag modernity and libs. We have to do something different to break away. We keep repeating who we were because we are not killing roots.

We can clear the bad sex forests of sexual harassment, sexual misconduct and sex crimes all we want. Burn it and burn it again. The roots are still there. The secrets, the lies, the half-truths and half-stories, the blame game and self-righteousness contribute to keeping gender inequality, sex crimes and racism, et al alive. We have yet to tell the whole truth and be comprehensive in our approach and our methodologies. If we really want Sexual Justice, Gender Equality and Social Justice, we may try something different – truth.

Ancient China

The Ancient China sex script was as diverse as its various empires and beliefs. In *Shaping a Nation*, the tentacles of sex culture are octopuses that touch every facet of a society; some aspects of society get locked in a vice grip of sex culture. To inspect a Monogamy with Flings (MFs) comprehensively, it is imperative to study the MF's effect on women, on men, on boys, on girls.

If your mother was a cook-clean-child-rearing sideline, it is likely that a girl learned that is what she was to be; it is likely that a boy learned that is what his mother was to be and consequentially, that is what his wife had to be. And yes, perhaps being a cook-clean-child-rearing sideline was a noble thing if someone or something could convince a woman of that, or if she was treated like that. How did the Monogamy with Flings "wife" explain the other women? A sign of wealth.

The Han Empire loved Mr. MF and men were in if they could afford the other women. Happy husband, happy life? The man was happy (or something). But what about the woman? [Sidebar: One may ask the same of our contemporaire, "Happy wife, happy life" idiom. i.e. "But what about the man?"]

Filial piety sounds so noble until the bell swings so far to the left, piety breeds chaos. Filial piety was revered in some ancient Chinese cultures. This cultural norm was the religious devotion to revering the family unit above all. Filial piety lost the love like most of our "religious" undertakings. When you have to place a girl infant under a bed to train her soul to be a slave to Superior, filial piety is a debilitating system that eats the humanity of those subjected to it. When you have to sacrifice a living human being to worship a dead ancestor in the name of filial piety, you have tipped the scales on the side of inhumane.

"We don't get to judge another's culture."

Culture respected, but is it good?

... And, about "judging" again. We've taken one word and used it to try to silence the masses. If indeed "judging" is bringing an issue to the table, it's fascinating that one cause, personality, hashtag or organization can do it to the rest of the world, but the rest of the populace cannot. In digging up roots and changing our current foul sex game, *discussing* all of the parts of us truthfully could shed some light on our present, prevailing sex shit. Sex shit that has thrived for years under the beds, in the damned closets and across continents.

So in the name of culture, Chen grew up in the darkness of under-the-bed and believed with all of her heart that she was indeed inferior and lesser. Some of us still believe we're inferior; hence, the vicious fight.

We've come a long way, Baby ...

If a girl learns to be a maid, then she will be a maid. There is nothing wrong with being a maid nor a queen if we respect the humanity of maid and queen. A maid is a job. It is not who he or she is. If we treat a maid less than queen because she is a maid, we've defined her by her job instead of by who she is – queen.

Here goes status and the way we think. We label people and many people believe they are what we label them. This is one of the reasons why we believe we are valuable or worthless. This is part of why we think we have to fight. Only you have to believe you are valuable. Killing the bastards to prove that you are valuable may be part of your necessary fight to believe in you, but you have to believe you're valuable because you are; not because the bastard is down with your stilettos in his throat.

If a boy learns that girls are maids and less than, he will treat them like that. If a girl learns that being a good wife is being prostituted out by her husband, she learns that "adultery" is normal. "Adultery" in quotes because in her sex cult-ure, sexing his transient business associates is normal. If she learns that his money is so important, it buys him the lifestyle and culture of The Other Women, she learns that normal.

Today, Chen brings hundreds of years of insecurities to the table of The Sex War with show-no-mercy for the men who taught her she was less than, even if it takes witchcraft to change the power play game to be in her favor. Being the wife of Mr. Monogamy with Flings is no longer a "beautiful life".

Anti-Aging or Eternal Life

Good sex has its benefits, but eternal life? Immortality? Sex equals eternal life sounds sacrilegious to people who believe eternal life will happen some other way but people believed they could "sex their way to immortality". That is one of the beauties of freedom of choice. We get to choose to believe and try all kinds of things; so that is what they did; we still do. They tried other things to have eternal life. For certain Daoists, sex was it – a way to have eternal life. May your way equal eternal life instead of eternal death. According to legend, this is how the first Chinese emperor lived forever – sexing thousands of virgins.

At fourteen, young virgins were prime for sex that enhanced a Dao man's vitality and equaled longevity. Today we call that sex with minors and pedophilia, but anyway... If her valuable virginity was lost at 14, does that mean she depreciates after 14 because he took her virginity? After eighteen (some believed) a virgin was pretty much over the hill to enhance the Dao man's vitality and extend his longevity.

Unfortunately, the Daoists who attempted to live forever via sex are dead. It seems as if sexing for eternal life failed. Nobody is living forever with these techniques. Please take note that no one is living forever with these techniques. Whatever they were, as secret as they may have been, those people are no longer here. Unfortunately some of us still haven't made this correlation – that sexing does not make us live forever. So we go at it to sex our way to immortality as if our sex thing will be any different than theirs.

Egypt and Sex: Then

As with all of our groups, sects and societies, someone always believed otherwise. While people were doing it "the right way" to have eternal life, others were not doing it: not even to have eternal life. Ancient Egypt took masturbation to procreation levels, incest was royalty and crocodiles were invaluable sex assets.

Sex File

While Ancient Egypt wasn't the only world where masturbation was a part of sex culture, their god of chaotic waters, Atem, masturbated his son and daughter into existence. Atem tapped his female side while masturbating Shu, his son, and Tefnut, his daughter, into being. His female side was his masturbating hand.

Incest was as prevalent as bloodlines; some cultures still have incest – hidden or overt. In Ancient Egypt incest was the choice of royalty. If royalty says, "You only sex your kind", a society follows suit. Royalty is still so hip. While science argues the effects of inbreeding on genetics and genetic disorders, King Tut's dynasty was plagued with several illnesses. Besides King Tut's cleft palate and curvature of the spine, his dynasty produced a boy king with degenerative bone disease. On the other hand, the Ptolemy dynasty seemed to escape illnesses. This did not contribute to the incest-genetic disorder belief but Ptolemy and Tut were not the only incest players.

If we could possibly tame a crocodile, sexing them may be more popular today. And, this walk on the wild side may be more attractive because it is so ... dangerous. In Ancient Egypt, maybe sexing a crocodile was about some level of prowess - it takes skill, wit, strength or other to finesse this beast into position and sex it, but crocodile sex was a part of some of Egypt's sex culture. Ode to the crocodile! Not only was it a sex partner, crocodile dung was used as a contraceptive.

Imagine us (if you dare). These are some of the more "civilized" cultures and this is a very short list of the sex stories of us. Consider the twists and flavors of Sex and Culture with all of our trillions of neurons trying what we believe behind closed doors. If we go to the prehistoric and ancients of countries and continents we would have exhaustive volumes of sex and sexuality as diverse as the billions of us that have graced the planet and now star in our current sex crises.

CHAPTER 60
THE SEX MELTING POT

And so we have this melting pot of sex, with humans colliding from every known continent, every rural dank, every venereal fusion, sexing to the tune of que sera. Uhhhhh, it's a couple minutes high, if that: for some, more. (For those who've mastered the art of erectile-potent moments, more like hours or so).

Let's go higher. Have a go at a hobby so beyond your rogue, it tops The 2-minute High. We have yet to tap another 1% of our potential. Beautiful sex is ours to enjoy. Enjoy it if it's all good, but if he's gagging to death in the chain contraption, maybe you should find something you haven't discovered yet to get a high. What is our vexation with sex? Why does it own us? Today we are in the hands of one of our masters – Sex. It is our master, for surely, we do not own it.

We think that we are ready for The Bad Sex Story. The world sits front and center to the stories of victims. We listen and we say. There are so many sides to The Bad Sex Story. The other sides are lost in the blood baths of The War on Sex; the war is the prevailing theme. Whatever minor deliberations on solutions are not so juicy. The Sex War lash out is merciless and the casualties are a toll on the human race that cost what we cannot pay. We may just have to start from somewhere we call HERE.

Where did all of this come from? Who cares? The table is set but it is a table that mainly empathizes with victims only. How did victims become victims? And again, where did all of this come from? The Bad Sex Story has a beginning: look at Prehistoric Sex: the ones we don't know about yet too and the ones we don't mention. Whether The Bad Sex Story will end depends on the writers. How it ends depends on the players.

If we trace our ancestries, we will find the beginning of The Bad Sex Story. And, they (their bad sex stories) really started before our ancestries as we know them. Women were without class, girls were married at puberty or sooner, animals were sex partners as long as they had an ass or genitalia and men were kingpin. Who cares? What does that have to do with the current sex war?

Culture, Sex Culture

The ghosts of sex past don't die. How to kill a ghost? Our progenitors have tried to clean up the physical aspects of how they sexed and some have even killed seed, but people always came back to what they did thousands of years ago. Our sex cultures still bear striking resemblances of what they did and some people still do what they did. These are high places – Untouchables by our mere human means - principalities, powers, demons. Ghosts don't die. And since we are hell bent on doing it MY way, our ghosts live on. Whatever progress we may make thrives on the spirit of what is foundational to us ... - sexual dysfunction, for the most part.

We only have to look at ancient China and Africa, et al, to find our Sex with Minors codes. We can see the old sex cultures of the American South in some of tribal Africa where girls as young as

12-years-old were christened into the world of sex by their mothers. By the age of 12, she knows how to please a man and be a wife. Young wives are as old as the Bible. We call it sex with minors. They call it normal. We can trace parts of tribal Africa's 12-year-old girls' sex culture to the old South, other regions and to current cultures.

We call it open and some of us call it adultery but Ancient China called it being hospitable to share his wife with the guest from abroad.

When our children sing the songs of sex with animals, they only echo our ancestors who sexed animals including riding the crocodile in Ancient Egypt. Here (in Ancient Egypt) the crocodile was not just for pleasure. Crocodile feces was invaluable for birth control.

You cannot put crocodile faeces on your vulva or in your vagina and maintain health. Crocodile faeces in your vagina will certainly cause disease; it's crocodile defecate. Today some of our birth controls rank with feces if we are honest enough to look at the recalls and class action lawsuits for cancer.

We are so much more sophisticated today with our plethora of contraception. And while we proudly say, that our birth control drugs do not cause ovarian, cervical, breast and other deadly cancers any more than other causes, no one has the wherewithal to explain why there are so many more cases of these inhumane diseases with the introduction of our modern contraceptives. The cause-and-effect cliché that so adequately explains so many of our life events suddenly does not apply to the world of our current birth control-reproductive system cancer crises.

Without some conscience, it is likely that humanity can drive some subset of its population to extinction. Nevermind that. Some of us care more about the Bornean orangutan on the endangered species list way more than we care if our daughters live or die. How ludicrous! Truth is ludicrous to many of us. We are driving some of us to extinction as we speak.

Cultures spread. Ancient Egyptian culture becomes American culture if Mr. American likes sex with his sister, a crocodile or the gods. We have come to America and we are trying to recreate a new culture of respect but we are trying to build on old foundations. We have our niceties of respecting another's culture and tolerance but have not communicated what is acceptable and what is not. Some things you just have to kill. Being nice to shit is tolerance for more shit. And unless we are willing to cut the head off of certain cultural practices that we have respect for, the demons will not die. It is mandatory to kill that. Keep the good and slay the bad.

We cannot tell Natasha from Malawi, I love your lips so it's okay to practice your 12-year-old girl sex initiation here and faint when Sex Culture is initiating your 12-year-old American daughter into their sex ranks. You cannot tell Song from China to bring her money and worship her designer bag and frown when she is swinging with your husband. And, so on... There are things non-negotiable. NO STEREOTYPE INTENDED in presenting any nation as our general perceptions portray: i.e. women from China are women not designer bag images, African women are women, and women from … are women.

Caveat: Many non-American sex cultures successfully adapt to American sex culture.

Bestiality, incest, prostitution, infidelity, open, rape, orgies ... the list goes on to an excruciating degree. Normalizing these cultures does not make them good.

Why does Mr. Sexual Harassment and Mrs. Adultery keep tripping over the same roots? Why does she choose the same abusive type? Why is her daughter doing the same? Your sex ghosts are now DNA. A computer is programmed to boot up to windows when you turn it on. You are programmed to that sex view. How to make it go away? How to change that? Change your code. How? It depends on how badly we want to change our codes – decode and reprogram.

Unfortunately, death is a viable option for some of us. Some of us would die doing it to say, "I did it my way".

CHAPTER 61
EXTRAMARITALS

Sex File

Today she sat on the sofa where she always did after her school pick-up. He tucked their children (ages 4 and 8) far enough away behind closed doors in their 8-year-old daughter's bedroom. Then he returned to the scene where they had most of their fights.

She was ready for him; the fighting was so banal, she knew how to ignore his taunting accusations about her affair. He knew how to incite her about his sidepiece but today it was different. Today they screamed their fight and the blows came as they always did. Today, she was blocking blows and fighting back but preoccupied with directing away her 8-year-old daughter's eyes. She was used to her parents' fights but her father had never tucked them away from the scene. The yelling and screaming brought her to peer around the wall in the hallway. This was normal to her but her mother's eyes ...

The first stab with the knife he wielded was shocking. It was not just another fight. To him, it was time to end it all. He cannot tell when she drew her last breath; his rage did not care. He did not feel his 8-year-old grabbing at his possessed arm to try and save her mother's bloody life. He could not hear 8-year-old screams neither. He flung his daughter away without even realizing she was there. The rage was his passion; his bloody wife on the floor his satisfaction. She was dead.

They don't all end this way. It doesn't matter – one is enough. The bludgeoned heart gets hardened but living with these crises is unacceptable.

It was an extramarital for them. As infidelity goes, it takes at least two but we're still biased to hanging the woman. A man is a man. In part, this is what fans the flames of our present merciless manhunt to take the bastards down – treating women unfairly. Why is it more accepted for a man to sidekick? Where is his wife? For the cheating wife, where is her husband? Whatever the cultures and the times, we are here. Unfortunately, the causes, organizations and hashtags have a show-no-mercy clause for sexual crimes.

Open relationship, swinging or multisexual, are we really happier? What are the price tags? If that is what you sign up for – open, swing, multisexual, polygamy - may the gods have mercy on you. The cultures of polygamists and concubines are in. If she didn't sign up to keep your cheat-sheet, what is your point? What is behind the heart of a man, a woman, who can go there? To adultery.

What brings a married cheater to another person's bed? No, not blame. We watch the shows and the tabloids and most of us stop at the juiciness of the story. What is it in our pasts? What is in her roots? In his? Really. Why is it not odious to sex his wife? Why is it thrilling to be pumping her husband? Is the sidekick getting off on the damage her cheating with her husband will do to her, or is it the adrenaline rush of stolen goods that makes the sex more saucy? There is a defective coding in there – especially if we enjoy it. Once? Twice, with guilt. But, another?

Watch her! She's got her eyes on you, Hubby. If it is only the devil inside or wanting dirty candy, there are women who have an unstoppable attraction to married men. What insecurity bred this? Work it out.

Like our first beer or glass of wine, if we can get over the buzz to where we can be social and cool about the libations, we think we're all grown up. This approach to his wife or her husband contributes to degradation in our society of kosher marital relations. Most of us have enough respect, (sense or conscience), not to steal his money or her car. Why is it okay to be casual about stealing someone else's husband or wife?

Nobody wants to look at their past places and root systems. We just want to destroy a bastard for being a bastard or a bitch for being bitchy. Tomorrow it will cost us too much because we refuse to look at the whole story. Once again, we're putting bandaids on an incurable.

Many suffer with Big Dog Lust disease. If ever you were an addict, drive on the other side of town from Dealer's house to get to work.... If you have a killer lust problem, work it out. If it's more wicked than you, there is grace for that, but you must want it.

Again someone is always slighted. Whether it's the faithful wife home with the kids, the husband, Ms. Fling trying to convince the husband to love her, or the lost kids. Most of the times, if Ms. Fling gets her hubby, she is still not satisfied. It's not the hubby she wanted. It's that place inside that needs to be fixed; the place that cannot be satisfied with our meagre things or our scandalous things – a victory win at stealing another's husband.

Are you really a "woman"? Face yourself.

Are you really a "man"? Man up and face yourself.

Defective Arrow is the picture of a defective heart. It is aimed and shot one way; instead, it goes another way: in a totally different direction than it is aimed and shot. We hesitate, refuse to or just neglect to fix the heart places. And if there were some other way around this other than fixing our hearts, we could take that route. The only substitutes for not addressing the human heart are vices - a more defective bent.

We continue to bring our little girl self into relationships and marriages for a man to love. (We don't even want to be fixed anymore.) We bring the lil' boy like he's coming home to his mama and when she tries to be his mama, he cringes. You cringe and find yourself a pussy because there is no way to sex your ma. You cannot make love to your mother. He cannot make love to you if you are treating him like you're his mother. You (both of you) may be able to step out of the mother-wife/little boy-husband role on a "horny" night, but in the morning, you're back to the mother and the little boy. Billy still needs his mama, but the man urges in him needs a pussy. Fix the little boy, Billy.

Little Boy Billy may not be your problem, Man. Why else would you rather sex someone other than your wife? It may be a power trip or a way to destroy your wife. In any event, there is a place of resolve. The place of resolve is where we decide that this – marriage – is what we want or don't want.

In a world where marriages are fleeting and longevity means 5-to-10 (years), we must decide what we're going in for before we bring her to the altar, the shoreline or the cliffs overlooking the mountains. Define it! Is it a forever thing or our new definition of longevity? If it's the new definition, get what you can from him before you go. Get that seed, Man! Where are we? Is that all that we are capable of? Maybe something was wrong with our grandparents – staying forever in half-ass marriages (some of them). Maybe, to be fair to him and to her, we need to define whatever our "marriage" thing is. For those who want a forever thing, get married at 70 or 80, marry Forever or get something that is a fringe benefit of an opulent success life. For those of us who are in it for the money, the tax benefits, the social, the fame or the status, forever is subject to that – fame, money, etceteras.

We confuse love with love. Loving people means respecting all of that person. The affair may feel good to you and her. And, maybe both of you can justify it. But, what about her husband: her children: her life? What about your children: your wife: your life? What about you?

Is that worth saving to you? - Your adultery marriage thing. It can be fixed. The question is, how badly do we want to fix our broken marriage things?

The sex is bigger than the sex and the "bad" that we label "cheating" is of the other kind. When you are bad by yourself, with yourself and for yourself, you only screw up yourself, directly; indirectly, we usually screw up someone else. To cheat is to explicitly screw yourself and them – your wife, your honey and/or your children.

If your extramarital sex sidekick can control you with that –sex, trinkets, money or mind games - he owns your soul. If she can control you with that, she owns you.

The media is rampant with sex for money. Ain' no shame in the game that Ms. Money had a fling with a married man. Nobody's really talking Her: She had a fling with a married man (if it is true).

The battle is about how to define the pay grades for sex tricks to shut her mouth. The talk is about how long $50K will shut her mouth versus $100K. Why do you think so little of yourself that you have to screw a married power player for money, Queen? You're more than that, Queen.

CHAPTER 62
HORNY

"Horny" is so ... It takes us so far away from the non-physical aspects of beautiful sex, it gives sex more of a raw physical vibe. It may work in the sex moments for turn on and lingo, but if we go back to the good root of us, we will still find sex is more than just physical. You will find that sex is good in its context.

The body beautiful. We are wired to have wonderful libido. There is a liberating place of embracing good sexuality instead of being ashamed or guilty because we have so many bad sex places. We may even go so far to say that we must exercise caution to maintain a healthy sense about good sex in our present atmospheres where groups and media are condemning bad sex. And some of us must deliberately defy the notion that desiring good sex is bad. Libido is wonderful. Libido is healthy. Don't let the onslaught on sex kill yours. What to do with the libidinous, though?

Plan one hell of a rendezvous.

Learn your hotspots.

Down boy!

What is healthy?

Once again, if you don't own that and cannot control that, check that. "Mind over matter", we say. We have the power to own our horny game. Again, back in the day, the sex free-for-all was not so free when a man had to consider that all of his children from all of his free-for-alls with different women had to fight for his inheritance. Today, our variety of birth control options limits the seed, but there is always something to check the horny if it needs to be checked. Find yours. We can get lost in the momentum of just going with our horny.

If you introduce pleasure of any kind to the human experience, at least one of us will exploit it.

Anal sex, oral sex, sex – what owns you? What is behind your thing? The art of living well is the art of balance that maintains wholeness – body, mind, soul, spirit. Sometimes balance may be a *good* sex night overboard.

It's powerful to discover that we are unbalanced in some way. It is freedom to conquer that – i.e. fix our imbalances.

Most of us have an emergency plan – for fire, for accidents, for financial disaster: for tornados or tsunamis: for hurricanes or floods. We even have pre-systems installed for fire – smoke alarms, extinguishers, away-from-home apps on our phones, Alexa. We don't wait for the emergency to get a plan. We try to prevent and take precautions to prevent. What's your plan for the roaring throes of raging, uncontrollable, lusty lust that makes you tremble?

Well, if you wait until Lusty Lust roars to have a plan, you will lose the lust game. Get a game plan.

What's better than sex?

What kills that libido, man?

Hater: Nobody wants their libido dead.

Nobody wants to live with the consequences of your sex rampage neither, unless it is your lover and you love him or her good. Holding the libido in check if the sex scenario is not good is a temporary solution for boom sex later.

What can you do now to be ready for serious boom sex later?

There is always something in life to top a moment in heat; but you cannot wait to be in heat to have a game plan.

"How do I WAIT with my flesh screaming with deep desire?"

Find something much better to do and have principles. Something much better may even be something bordering on immediate crisis or in the full throes of crisis to shock the body and the mind out of the sex passion.

Literally? Breathe deeply to pace that physical pant passion. Literally? Cold shower if that works – the restless mind too. Literally, plan a sex date for all parameters to be good later.

"What about when you want sex so badly? You want it bad."

Is it good? Are all the parameters good? We want the billion dollars badly too. How do we get it? Is stealing it good?

"Yeah, the money and the sex pull on two different desires."

How do you control yourself from stealing a million dollars?

"It's not the same."

The will kicks in or a strategy. If all the parameters are good for a good beautiful sex rendezvous, by all means rendezvous away. If all the parameters are not good, you'd better kick-in the will, the mind and/or a chastity belt with locks and keys.

The physical body does its thing when hormonal urges and sex passions knock. How do you respond? Answer if it's all good. If it's not all good, submit to your will (no matter how illicit the moment is). If you are at its whim it owns you.

The Urge to Splurge

We have a tendency to let-you-be-you. Except for certain presidents and high profile personalities – who must be how everyone tells him or her to be – it's okay to be whatever. Discipline is for Olympiads; and they only have to be disciplined at their sport. Respect is that old song, R-E-S-P-E-C-T: if we've even heard of the song. Wait is for the server at our favorite food joint. And, self-help means help yourself to the biggest booty, his bank or his company. So, if we want to sex 10 people (or things) a night, play a sex-circle of 300 all around the world this year or 50 within the L.A. basin, we go for it.

One of the problems with this "freedom", is it is a fake. Fake freedom is really a high-road to places on the Unwanted Bucket List. When you're a slave to anything, it owns you.

We scoff at the addict. If you listen to the story of any addict, you will hear a life out of control in some way. Sexing like that is the same. What's your story, Man? What's your story, Beautiful?

Be good to you.

You will always want more. That is inherently in us. We cannot help but want more. Love is a beautiful thing. Splurge on it. Find someone worth loving and splurge on love with him or her. You may have to find Jesus on this one - to splurge on love with. Everyone is not worthy of your love splurge. Or take a chance on the "unworthy", if you dare. Love vested pays dividends nonpareil.

Freedom is when you own you.

Work out The Horny.

CHAPTER 63
MASTURBATION

Atem – "the creator and finisher of the world" - created Shu and Tefnut by spitting them out of his mouth; masturbation is used to describe this reproduction process. How? His masturbating hand represented his inner female principle.

Atem – the Egyptian god of war

This idea of a sole creator is an attempt to "parallel" Christianity's paternal deity relationship between God and Jesus (God's Son) in that Jesus is the only begotten son of God. One of the differences is, Atem had two children instead of one. Maybe he only masturbated twice.

Unlike Atem, the Christian God does not have to masturbate to create. He speaks. So far, human has not arrived to such a power: the ability to masturbate to reproduce. Anyway, Atem was the father of Egypt's king. With stories like these, a king ruled a nation – the most powerful nation of its time.

Whereas most settle for the pleasures of masturbation, this philosophical take on masturbation is more spiritual. Once again, we can trace our today to yesterday; although no one needs an

Egyptian god to discover the pleasure of touch. Atem took the masturbation principle to another level.

Masturbation is not sex and has yet to produce offspring. So, what is it? Is it just an attempt to stop the raging bull that wants sex? Is it the power to feel so alive? Or, perhaps it's just about pleasure. And, maybe, the saddest thought is the fact that you do not have someone to touch you like that, if you don't.

It is a beautiful pleasure to discover what feels good to us and oh the exhilaration of orgasms! The journey to a moment of pleasure can be as anticipating as a weekend with our #1. Sexy masturbation has taken the mind to a place where it is free and for a brief moment the present is lost in sweet oblivion. How to stay in such sweet oblivion places? Or, is the moment as fleeting as the last Decadent Chocolate Truffles that gave us a bliss? Do we have another Decadent Chocolate Truffles or worry about "a moment on the lips, forever on the hips"? Overwhelming are the pleasure places that turn into death traps because he went too far. And so, masturbation (and even sex) begs us look at what is really happening inside of us and what is behind the scenes of us.

There are some of us who will never get enough. The last high is never enough. We always need something more. At the end of the sigh of relief or disappointment, what do we have? If we do not tap our insatiable, Insatiable can kill. It has. Many people find themselves on the other side at the end of their masturbation or in the process of getting to some dangerously happy place. What are we really trying to satisfy? If something is missing, what is it?

Some of our societies and cultures make masturbation such a foul thing. And like our coy sex codes, if we buy into "masturbation is so foul", we live like Shame. Deeper than all of our coy and codes is: It is flabbergasting that in a world of approximately 8 billion people, we are still sometimes so alone or deprived; even the "lucky" or "damned" who have someone and still finds themselves alone ...; so alone that the human soul still screams, "Touch me, lest I die!"

Ahh! And, so it is, that we are ever searching for more than what is presented to us. Whatever gaping craters leave us writhing emotionally, physically, or spiritually for more – sex, pleasure, or thrills – are evidences of who we really are; or are not. When the physical touch is over, we are still empty, searching and needy. We need another fix, another high, another thrill. Don't let this be about shame. Desire is a part of what makes us alive. We were created this way. The Manufacturer was intentional in His design. It is not a design defect nor a manufacturing flaw that we are ever wanting and demanding more. Unfortunately, your best sex man cannot give that to you. She will never be enough for you.

One of our greatest mistakes is expecting for him or her or that to fix the chasm. She cannot fix the God-sized crater in us; neither can he or it. When the masturbation is over and the sex and the highs come down, we are still reaching. If we find our thing in making the next million or winning the next race, after the next million and the next win, we will still be reaching. That thing in us that screams, "Touch me lest I die!", is the untappable instinct of eternity.

Life is more than the 9-to-5's and making it big. It is more than the well-rounded of us who may have it all together. When Gerry makes love to his wife, he revels in that uncanny aspect of it that makes him feel wickedly alive! In "Dying for Love", Bruce would make love to his wife's lifeless body because he knew that is where they tapped a fountain of life so drastically vivid, they transcended the mediocrity of tangible existence. Perhaps, this is our pursuit. The pleasures of sex, of masturbation, of whatever high are just the side effects of the main event. Our instinct is to tap the untappable. We give up though and settle for meagre earthliness.

Do you wonder what would happen if we tapped just 5% more of our potential in madly good activity? Don't settle for just the 7-minute masturbation or sex high. Go for broke and *whoosh* past the reach to what is really aching inside – to be greater than just great. You are just a smidgen away from tapping another 1% of the untappable.

Or find something that fills the insatiable.

CHAPTER 64
INTO YOU

Fundamentally, something got lost in our very basic misunderstanding of woman, of man. We begin our early journeys of life not "getting" boys: we certainly don't "get" girls. Many of us don't "get" ourselves, yet we try to be with someone. Fundamental to sex is someone else - real sex. Fundamental to serious sex is loving someone you send reeling in a good way: someone who is worth you sending reeling. If you don't know him, if you don't know her, inherently, intrinsically, instinctively, the fundamentals are inadequate.

You cannot fully know something you do not love. You cannot fully love something you do not know.

Know is intimacy on superior levels.

She is what she is inside – good woman. He is what he is inside – good man. Not the inside that we succumb to. The inside that is our higher noble self. Inside, She is woman – good. Inside, He is man – good. Inside is who we are instinctively, intrinsically, inherently. If you kill his man or her woman – what and who, he or she is inside – there is no way to learn it. There is no way to love it. There is no way to sex it.

Do you know her? Yes, her! The woman you're sleeping with.
Do you even know her? Let's not go to the sex part of knowing
her. Do you know HER? The heart of her. If he wants to be
mesmerized with the heart of her, the physique of her may be just a
place to start.

Do you know the real color of her hair, her eyes? Why is it
naturally that color? Why does she prefer auburn instead of her
natural chocolate brown? Where did her natural chocolate brown
come from? What other ways would you describe that color
brown? Is there a gem that color? Which gem? What genetic
coding determines that her hair is cacao brown? Is it her Mother's
side or her father's side? Is it naturally straight, curly or wavy?
Why does it wind tighter into curls when it is wet? What can she
use for a better detangler? What is in it? Where do you get it for
her? Be that into her and go for her heart.

Do you know him? The hottie you're sleeping with. Does he have
his mother's lips? Why do his lips curl like that when he is angry
or frustrated? What frustrates him? How do you make it better?
Does his father's lips curl like that when he is angry too? Why
does he sing just before dinner? That same tune. He sings that
same tune just before dinner. Did you notice? What is that tune?
Why does he sing "Moonlit Lover" just before dinner? Do you
know that that is what his mother sang when she was preparing
dinner from he was sleeping in his basinet at the scent of beef
brisket or Tuesday Taco Night? Why did she hum that? Was it a
story in her past? Did she change the song from the story in her
past to "Color of Sunlight is You" as an empty nester? What else
does he remember about her? How does that affect your thing?
Does he need to get over that? Does it make your world with him
sexier? Be that into him. Go for the heart of him.

If you hate *that* thing about him that much, walk away from him before you accept his ring. If you can't get over her nuances, shortfalls and things that much, walk away from her before the ring thing: before the "I do". Figure out you. Maybe that is where we should all start - figuring out me. There are things about you that you may never figure out. Do we stop living at our stuck places? Many times the answers come in the journey; even if it's a lover who can love you through that, with that and in that; even a lover who can help you with that.

Lip Curls

What does his story have to do with you? We only mentioned his lip curl. We didn't even touch his practically-missing-eyebrow thing, or his love for flannel pajamas instead of cotton striped.

What about his foot fetish, his tobacco-scented cologne ingredient list, his heat rash in the summer and winter-clear skin?

Do you wonder how come he has a fear of heights but has a dream to fly a jetliner?

Did you even know he had such a dream? Why? Why is that his dream?

Ever surprised him with flying lessons?

"Can't afford it", she says.

Are you saving for it?

"There are more important things."

What is more important than his dreams?

What is more important than her dreams?

Oh Frivolous One! Who in the world cares about all of these things? Who cares about dreams?

If you can't find someone that into you, don't settle. If you're not that into her, leave her alone. Find someone you can love like that. When a man prefers his booze, his buddies and, or, his bag o' tricks over you, check him. If only we understood the value of beautiful sex that comes from love that romances a human heart. Such cheesy talk is what we have chalked love up to. And, so we wonder why our sex things and relationship things are so boring, shitty, non-existent, or _______________. The beauty of needing someone is that it makes us vulnerable. There is nothing casual about vulnerability. Vulnerability is frightening, especially for our independent selves. It's easier to wear our relationship masks. Needing is not the goal. Wanting someone comes from whole places. Even wanting him must be balanced with happy success with or without him.

If all you are about is his few dollars for your annual makeup and beauty kits, you're setting yourself up. If you're just into his bank, your god is flawed. You will always be a slave to it (big money god). Love him like that or leave him alone and go love yourself.

We haven't even started to talk about the sex part of what it is about her in bed? When you're that into someone, you have something. When you love someone like that, you have access to sex like that. Few of us even have access to sex and intimacy. So we cannot judge sex. As long as we settle for what takes us further away from who we really are – image of God - we will resort to perversion and extremes to feed the insatiable flesh. That is what insatiable is, Sexy. You cannot satisfy that. It will always want something more: something more extreme: something that takes you to the direct opposite side of opulent success. You cannot satisfy flesh. Recalibrate your sex palate. Recalibrate.

CHAPTER 65
VOLUPTUOUS

There once was a place called Voluptuous. A perfect, sexy man lived there with his badass queen.

Voluptuous was a place of giddy pleasure so blithe and abundant, it flowed rivers of gold. This is The Kingdom of Sex. Research that. Find that! If and when you do, then you have the foundations for some serious sex.

Voluptuous is a place where she begs a kiss from him with the kisses of his mouth. His love is better than wine, you see.

DAMN.

1. He's supposed to be loving you with a love that is better than your choice intoxicator.
2. She's supposed to evoke such desire in him. Not because she does but because she is.
3. You're supposed to feel that when he kisses you.
4. The Lover who created love and is love, is into loving, sex and intimacy like that.

If we tell you you're sex royalty, you can possibly believe and act like it long enough to change your bent.

You're sex royalty.

Oh, if we could see us! If only we could see us! You have no idea who you are. We have no idea who we are. You are a king! You are a queen! Not our kings and queens as we think of them. They are beautiful and some are honorably noble. You are royalty on a level that so far exceeds human comprehension. You are unprecedentedly sexy, Man! We do all of our games and power struggles and sex plays and desperation. And the more extreme we are, the more insatiable we are. We deviate so far in the other direction, we hit points of no return that rob us of ever discovering our true identity.

We were born with eternity in our hearts. Go after the master king that you are! Go after your noble identity! Is that your best you? Not weight, physique, hair, skin and nails? What are you running from to go to the next level of sex, greed, power? Like a painkiller, narcotics, prescriptions or gamebox, you will always need another level, and another, and another. What exactly is the real problem? It's okay to work it out. Work it Out! Work it out, but don't step further into that. Live! Live free. If that owns you, that is life on slavery. The art of living the best of us is lost in our fears.

Interested: How do I work it out?

You're a king. You're a queen.

"Those are some of the most screwed up people on the planet."

No. I mean, you're a queen. Diva Queen knows who she is. Not the titles, the throne and the authority, Diva Queen knows who she is inside. A king is a king inside. King will survive this sex war because he owns his game.

CHAPTER 66
YOUR SEX FILE

What does your sex file say? Is it a story of a premium life, lived well? Or is it a tragedy of damned codes from yesterdays? We have indelible pictures of horrific sex files and billions of blasé ones. There are few sex files rampant with sex that taps superior love codes. We can change our sex files at any time.

Who has ever made sweet love to your mind and your soul at the same time? Mmmm. Does he engage your body, mind and soul when he is not sexing you? If she is not touching you, does she consume your mind and your will? Who does that for you? Anyone? Oh, this is not honeymoon stage! This is it.

Our collective sex files mandate that we start over. We must scrap our sex DNA. We must trade our collective sex DNA for the sex genetics of the Sex Kingdom that we really belong to. This requires us to change perspectives to who we really are. It is quite natural to live something more that tends to sex utopia but, of course, we cannot do it with that attitude. It is shocking (but commonplace) that the utopia critics have no idea about what makes life utopic. Unfortunately, we believe them more than the sex creator who designed a world of voluptuous pleasure. If the designer designed a world of excessive pleasure, illicitly phenom sex is not the phantom that we make it to be. It is.

With all of our faculties, we harness the sun's energy, fly rockets to the galaxies, bounce communications off satellites to connect from one end of the earth to the next. But we fail to engage all of our faculties to arrive at some place where sex is unprecedentedly voluptuous. If we do not engage all our faculties on a quest to discover the world of voluptuous sex, we cannot discover the world of such voluptuous sex. If we do not believe that such a world exist, we will not seek it. What do we have to lose? The critics of voluptuous sex or a life of opulent success have no metrics to measure the possibility of sex like that or life like that. How dare we believe them! Like a resolution, try. At this point, we have nothing to lose. We've tried so many things. Thousands of years later, we are here. We know what we have – harassment, kill the bastards, disease, failed human relations. Why not try something else?

It is futile to embark on such journeys with anyone who lives less than sex royalty. We are all royalty. We are all sex royalty but most of us believe otherwise, so we live that way. Why believe the critic who lives less than sex royalty? Our sex files can only get better if we choose the sex royalty route. What's wrong with a sexy sex file? We embrace a lifestyle change for health, for wealth, for success. Why not embrace a lifestyle change for sexy Sex Kingdom sex?

Start with you. Love you like that. You're sex royalty. Let's change our sex files, rewrite our sex stories and create a badass sex DNA that is evident of the Kingdom of Sex. Sexually, that is where we're from.

AUTHOR PAGE

Selem Demwuth means image and likeness. We hold within us the image and likeness of Omniscient, Omnipresent, Omnipotent Authority.

The pen name "Selem Demwuth" was used to remind humanity about who we are and about the power of being who we are. It is unimaginable the power, the glory, the good impact of a human race that lives something worthy of the image and likeness of God.